The Fern Guic

A field guide to the ferns, clubmosses, quillworts and horsetails of the British Isles

Third Edition

By James Merryweather

Illustrated by Michael Hill, Carol Roberts and James Merryweather

First published 1992, 2nd edition 1995, 3rd edition 2007

ISBN: 978 185153 228 5
OP117.

Acknowledgements

Over the many years during which this book developed other people became involved in the project. A major contributor was Yvonne Golding, a York undergraduate who became official bully to author and illustrator (Michael Hill), making us get on with the job when we felt least enthusiastic about it.

Inspiration came from sundry sources. The members of the British Pteridological Society who taught me (JM) ferns from 1968, following my initiation by the late Edward Step (*Wayside & Woodland Ferns*, 1909). Jimmy Dyce MBE, of course, stands out as the great enthusiast and teacher, but in addition I would like to name a few others without whom pteridology would have not been nearly as much pleasure: Fred Jackson, Reg Kaye, Francis and Barbara Tingey, Clive Jermy, Martin and Hazel Rickard, Tony Worland, Marjorie Castellan, Margaret Kingston, Henry Schollick, Matt Busby, Jack Bouckley, Barry Thomas, Chris Page, Margaret Rothwell, Alison Rutherford and a host of other pteridomane friends. Sadly, some of them are no longer with us.

I always had a feeling that the way I learned from them should be available to others and, in 1976 the idea was put to the test by Dr. Andy Hodges, a zoologist with a desire to know more of botany. For him I put together a friendly key that seemed to work adequately. Nothing further happened to it until 1983 when, thanks to a chance gift from Brian Coles of a little American book – *Fern Finder*, I could see the way to produce a key to help inspire new, especially young, pteridologists and my hearty thanks go to its authoresses Anne and Barbara Hallowell, whose style was a major source of inspiration. It took a long time, but thanks to the FSC and Steve Tilling's faith in the project, *The Fern Guide* eventually came into being. This 3rd edition has been constructed thanks to enthusiastic support from Steve's successor Bek Farley. Once in print, *The Fern Guide* became the foundation of courses at FSC Centres, notably Blencathra, Orielton and Rhyd-y-Creau. The participants on those courses played a vital role in testing, correcting and fine-tuning the keys. I owe them all a huge debt of gratitude, not only for the improvements that have been incorporated in this edition, but also for the fun we all had, learning together in lab and field.

Contents

Introduction

Ferns have no colourful flowers, so why do some folk consider them to be so beautiful? I have no straightforward answer, but there can be no doubt that I and many others are irresistibly attracted to them, and even the other plants sharing the common feature of lacking flowers. All pteridophytes, as they are known to botanists, reproduce by spore rather than by seed in a life cycle described below. Other groups such as the algae, mosses and liverworts, also reproduce by releasing millions of minute wind- or water-borne spores to disperse afar and continue the existence of their species. The main contributor to the life of the plant is the generation which is dedicated to sexual reproduction – the gametophyte. However, the reproductive gametophyte is a small and – to us humans – insignificant flake of tissue known as the prothallus. In fact, the life-cycles of ferns, and their allies – the clubmosses, horsetails and quillworts – are dominated by the sporophyte (Fig. 1). The showy fronds of ferns, and the various leafy shoots of their allies, bear spore-production organs.

The ferns and their allies are ancient, appearing in the fossil record around four hundred million years ago. There are marked differences between the six main groups because, although they all retain the means of reproduction evolved by their distant ancestors, their vegetative states diverged markedly over the millenia. Today, Britain has six creeping clubmosses, three rush-like quillworts, eight horsetails with their jointed stems and whorled branches and 59 ferns, both plain and lacy-leaved (including adders tongues and moonwort though their relationship is very distant). These are only a fraction of the world's diversity, which itself is but a small remnant of the Pteridophyta of past eras.

This key is intended for use in the field, where its subjects grow naturally. It is hoped that the reader can get to understand and enjoy ferns without damaging them and the places where they grow. Please don't dig them up or pick more material than is necessary. Rarities must be left strictly as found to ensure their survival.

Pteridophyte life-cycles

These plants have recognisable leaves, stems and roots but they do not have flowers or seeds. Their reproductive structures evolved long before the flowers and the pteridophyte method of procreation has remained essentially the same for millions of years. As we have seen above, the pteridophytes in fact exist in two physical forms: the very obvious green, vegetative spore-producing generation responsible for species maintenance and dispersal (the sporophyte), and a tiny sexual reproductive phase known as the gametophyte (see Fig. 1). The conspicuous sporophyte takes many forms as this guide will show, for it is this part of the life cycle which is recognisable in the field. The tiny gametophyte (the prothallus), will be unfamiliar to most people; indeed, in some groups it is subterranean and unlikely to be encountered. The fern prothallus is to be found in moist places resembling a small liverwort or a filamentous alga. If fertilisation has occurred, it will bear a recognisable miniature fern, nurtured by the prothallus in its early growth. Since the main groups of the pteridophytes are evolutionarily quite distinct, it is not surprising that they differ in appearance. However, there are also major differences within the true ferns. Although the great majority display variations on the lacy-leaf theme there are many species which, at a glance, resemble anything but the accepted 'model fern'. The drawings on page 20 illustrate the range of forms which can be encountered.

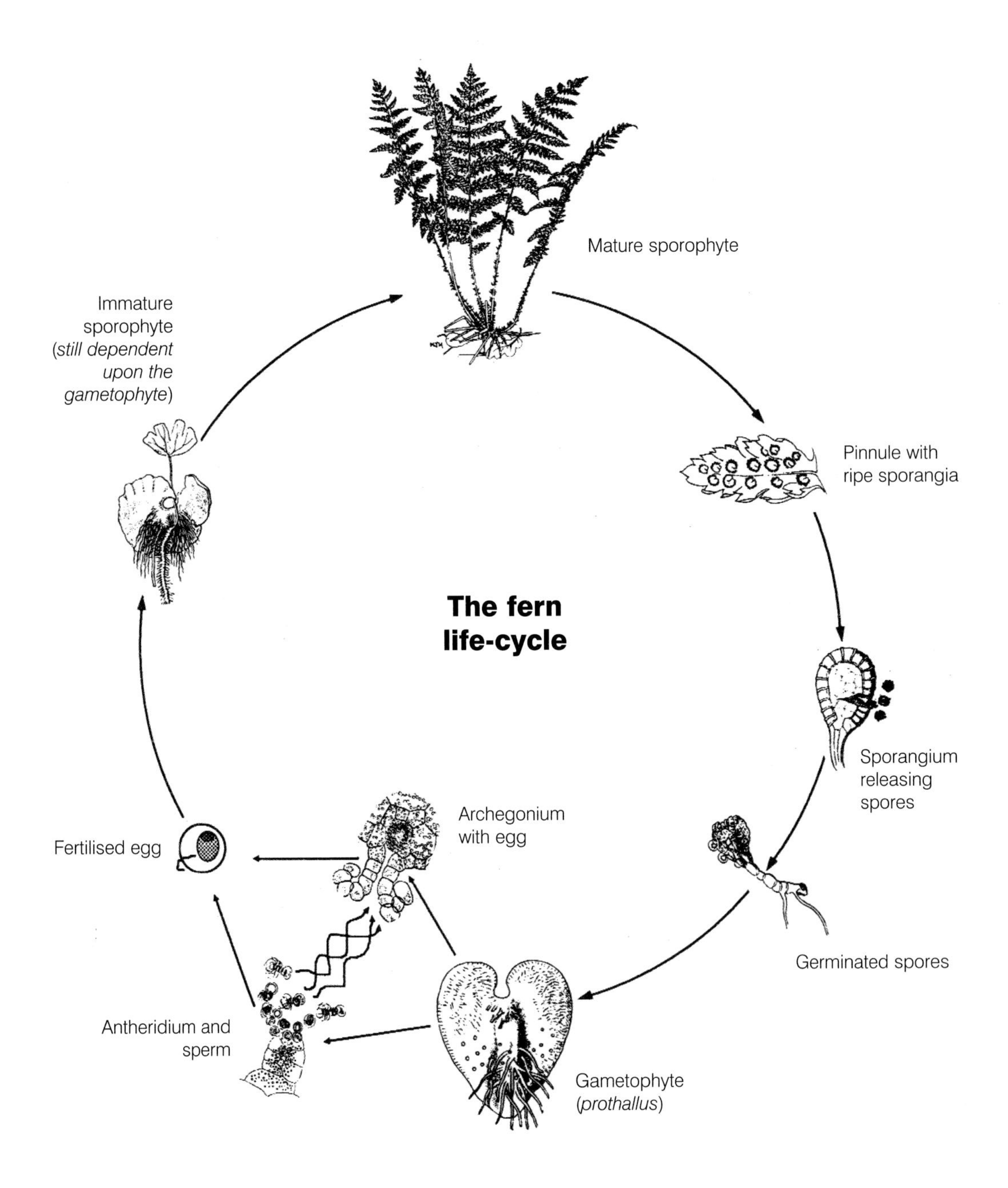

Figure 1. Most British pteridophytes are homosporous with a life-cycle such as illustrated here. The heterosporous species differ by having separate male and female spores and separate gametophytes.

Habitats

The ferns and their allies are found in most natural habitats: mountains, moorland, sand dunes, cliffs, grassland, streams, bogs and woods as well as on walls, along way-sides and in hedgerows. They can be common and two native species are, in fact, positive pests: the field horsetail *Equisetum arvense* of garden, field and allotment, and bracken *Pteridium aquilinum*, a woodland plant which is invading valuable moors, mountain pasture and arable land. However, although the pteridophytes are ancient plants they are, on the whole, in a state of evolutionary and ecological decline. Many are very rare, a function of habitat pressures and species losses worldwide.

How to use this guide

Like other AIDGAP publications, this guide is intended as an introductory key to a group of organisms whose identification can present beginners with substantial difficulty. Although the content of the guide is comprehensive, covering all the ferns and their allies encountered in the British Isles, the author accepts that it will not provide all the answers that a keen beginner will seek. When I first took a lone interest, armed with my copy of Edward Step's *Wayside and Woodland Ferns*, I could cope with a few very distinctive ferns such as the hard fern, hart's tongue and polypody, and felt that the "Dryopteris-like" ferns and the horsetails would never be possible. It was only with the help of more experienced botanists that I gained the courage to proceed. I found such people in the British Pteridological Society and I am sure that membership cannot be too highly recommended (see *Further information*).

Absolute confidence that your unidentified specimen is covered by this book will only come with experience, but it will be hastened if you have the good fortune to be in the company of a pteridologist or if you have access to a named collection. Each of the keys in the guide is introduced with a montage of possible forms which should help to keep you on the correct track. Familiarise yourself with the range of forms which can be encountered by flicking through the illustrations. However, don't try identifying your specimen by picture matching – you will almost certainly come unstuck. Here are some simple guidelines that will help you to name your specimen:

Select an adult fern

Ensure that you are looking at a mature plant. Juveniles are common but can be very difficult to identify with certainty in the field. You are advised to avoid immature specimens until you are familiar with adults (usually characterised by stature and the presence of sporangia). Later, similarities between known adults and doubtful juveniles may be compared, along with consideration of habitat and frequency of all possible parents.

KEY A – The Major Groups
If your specimen doesn't look like either of the first two species go to page 17 and begin the key to the four major pteridophyte groups. You are offered a detailed description of each. Choose the appropriate one and this will guide you to the name of the group to which your specimen belongs and to the key for that group.

The main keys
You have now been directed to a key which, by offering you options in pairs will lead you step by step to the identity, description and illustration of your specimen.

Observe all features
Whilst looking for the features you are required to recognise at each pair of choices (couplet), also be aware of the growth habit and ecological and geographical facts which may help you gain a full understanding of the pteridophyte in question.

Help
There is a main glossary of scientific terms (page 9) and a generalised structure diagram precedes each key to a major group. Do not be afraid of the few scientific terms you are required to tackle. These could be important additions to your vocabulary which will allow you to communicate concisely. If you are baffled by a scientific term, refer to the glossary for help.

Magnification 🔍
Occasionally, you will be required to use a hand lens to observe important semi-microscopical features. The purchase of a lens with a magnification of x10 is recommended. You can also obtain double lenses with the combinations: x8/x15 and x10/x20. I favour the latter. In the keys the 🔍 symbol will advise when use of the lens is required.

Conservation and the Law
Lastly, please be considerate. This book is intended for use in the field where its subjects grow naturally and I hope that you will be able to understand and enjoy ferns and their allies without damaging them or the places where they grow. Please don't dig them up; pick material only when it is absolutely essential and mind where you put your feet. Remember, not only is it highly undesirable to pick or dig up plants, it is illegal unless you have the permission of the land-owner. Many species of rare plant are totally protected by the law and prosecution can follow wilful damage to plant or habitat. If you wish to grow your own ferns, they may be purchased at Garden Centres (usually mislabelled and tatty, but a few are there nonetheless), or from one of the few specialist nurseries where excellent specimens are to be had. Alternatively, grow your own from spore. The British Pteridological Society is the place to find the experts and several excellent publications about fern culture (see *Further information*). You can easily collect your own spores or dip into the huge variety available from the Society's spore exchange.

A Checklist of the Ferns and Other Pteridophytes of the British Isles

The taxonomy of the pteridophytes is constantly under review, in tandem with progress in understanding of their biology, evolution and relationships. Unfortunately, this means that nomenclature changes are inevitable. Sooner or later, some names will change again. This may, at first, seem terribly inconvenient, but it (usually) serves us well by improving the accuracy with which we communicate with each other about pteridophytes, and share advances in knowledge.

Hybrids – the ones so far discovered – are listed here so that you may be aware of the range of possible crosses which might cause some difficulty when you encounter them. Only one hybrid can be considered to be at all common: *Polypodium* x *mantoniae* is frequently found in the regions where its parents' ranges overlap, especially in the south-west. It is a very robust plant which may survive as huge colonies in places where the parents have long disappeared. Others (which are found more often as one becomes acquainted with their parents!) are *Dryopteris* x *deweveri* and *Equisetum* x *littorale,* which may be found in the vicinity of their parents, intermediate in both appearance and habitat. Full descriptions of all British pteridophyte species and hybrids may be found in Page, 1997.

DIVISION: LYCOPHYTA

CLUBMOSSES
ORDER LYCOPODIALES
FAMILY Lycopodiaceae
Lycopodium annotinum L. **Interrupted clubmoss**
Lycopodium clavatum L. **Stag's horn clubmoss**
Lycopodiella inundata (L.) Holub **Marsh clubmoss**
Huperzia selago (L.) Bernh. ex Schrank & Mart. **Fir clubmoss**
Diphasiastrum alpinum (L.) Holub **Alpine clubmoss**

SPIKEMOSSES
ORDER SELAGINELLALES
FAMILY Selaginellaceae
Selaginella selaginoides (L.) P. Beauv. ex Schrank & Mart. **Lesser clubmoss**

QUILLWORTS
ORDER ISOËTALES
FAMILY Isoëtaceae
Isoëtes echinospora Durieu **Spring quillwort**
Isoëtes histrix Bory **Land quillwort**
Isoëtes lacustris L. **Common quillwort**

DIVISION: MONILOPHYTA

HORSETAILS
ORDER EQUISETALES
FAMILY Equisetaceae
Equisetum arvense L. **Field horsetail**
Equisetum fluviatile L. **Water horsetail**
Equisetum hyemale L. **Dutch rush** or **rough horsetail**

Equisetum palustre L. **Marsh horsetail**
Equisetum pratense Ehrh. **Shade horsetail**
Equisetum sylvaticum L. **Wood horsetail**
Equisetum telmateia Ehrh. **Great horsetail**
Equisetum variegatum Schleich. ex F. Weber & D. Mohr. **Variegated horsetail**

HYBRIDS
Equisetum x *moorei* Newman [*E. hyemale* x *E. ramosissimum*]
Equisetum x *trachyodon* A. Braun [*E. hyemale* x *E. variegatum*]
Equisetum x *dycei* C.N. Page [*E. fluviatile* x *E. palustre*]
Equisetum x *littorale* Kühlew. ex Rupr. [*E. arvense* x *E. fluviatile*]
Equisetum x *mildeanum* Rothm. [*E. pratense* x *E. sylvaticum*]
Equisetum x *bowmanii* C.N. Page [*E. sylvaticum* x *E. telmateia*]
Equisetum x *font-queri* Rothm. [*E. palustre* x *E. telmateia*]
Equisetum x *robertsii* Dines [*E. arvense* x *E. telmateia*]
Equisetum x *rothmaleri* C.N. Page [*E. arvense* x *E. palustre*]
Equisetum x *willmotii* C.N. Page [*E. fluviatile* x *E. telmateia*]

ADDER'S TONGUES & MOONWORT
ORDER OPHIOGLOSSALES
FAMILY Ophioglossaceae
Botrychium lunaria (L.) Sw. **Moonwort**
Ophioglossum azoricum C. Presl **Small adder's tongue**
Ophioglossum lusitanicum L. **Least adder's tongue**
Ophioglossum vulgatum L. **Common adder's tongue**

FERNS
ORDER FILICALES
FAMILY Osmundaceae
Osmunda regalis L. **Royal fern**

FAMILY Adiantaceae
Adiantum capillus-veneris L. **Maidenhair fern**
Anogramma leptophylla (L.) Link **Jersey fern**
Cryptogramma crispa (L.) R. Br. **Parsley fern**

FAMILY Marsileaceae
Pilularia globulifera L. **Pillwort**

FAMILY Hymenophyllaceae
Hymenopyllum tunbrigense (L.) Sm. **Tunbridge filmy fern**
Hymenophyllum wilsonii Hook **Wilson's filmy fern**
Trichomanes speciosum Willd. **Killarney bristle fern**

FAMILY Polypodiaceae
Polypodium cambricum L. **Southern polypody**
Polypodium interjectum Shivas **Western polypody**
Polypodium vulgare L. **Common polypody**

HYBRIDS

Polypodium x mantoniae Rothm. [*P. interjectum* x *P. vulgare*]
Polypodium x shivasiae Rothm. [*P. cambricum* x *P. interjectum*]
Polypodium x font-queri Rothm. [*P. cambricum* x *P. vulgare*]

FAMILY Dennstaedtiaceae

Pteridium aquilinum (L.) Kuhn **Bracken**
Pteridium pinetorum C.N. Page & R.R. Mill **Pinewood bracken**

FAMILY Thelypteridaceae

Thelypteris palustris Schott **Marsh fern**
Oreopteris limbosperma (Bellardi ex All.) Holub **Mountain** or **lemon scented fern**
Phegopteris connectilis (Michx.) Watt **Beech fern**

FAMILY Aspleniaceae

Asplenium adiantum-nigrum L. **Black spleenwort**
Asplenium ceterach L. (*Ceterach officinarum* Willd.) **Rusty-back fern**
Asplenium marinum L. **Sea spleenwort**
Asplenium obovatum Viv. subsp. *lanceolatum* P. Silva **Lanceolate spleenwort**
Asplenium onopteris L. **Western black spleenwort**
Asplenium ruta-muraria L. **Wall rue**
Asplenium scolopendrium L. (*Phyllitis scolopendrium* (L.) Newman) **Hart's tongue fern**
Asplenium septentrionale (L.) Hoffm. **Forked spleenwort**
Asplenium trichomanes L. subsp. *trichomanes* **Delicate maidenhair spleenwort**
Asplenium trichomanes subsp. *quadrivalens* D.E. Mey. **Common maidenhair spleenwort**
Asplenium trichomanes subsp. *pachyrachis* (Christ) Lovis & Reichst. **Lobed maidenhair spleenwort**
Asplenium viride Huds. **Green spleenwort**

HYBRIDS

Asplenium x *confluens* (T. Moore ex E.J. Lowe) Lawalrée [*A. scolopendrium* x *A. trichomanes*]
Asplenium x *tichense* D.E. Mey [*A. adiantum-nigrum* x *A. onopteris*]
Asplenium x *sarniense* Sleep [*A. adiaintum-nigrum* x *A. obovatum* subsp. *lanceolatum*]
Asplenium x *jacksonii* (Alston) Lawalrée [*A. adiantum-nigrum* x *A. scolopendrium*]
Asplenium x *contrei* Callé, Lovis & Reichst. [*A. adiantum-nigrum* x *A. septentrionale*]
Asplenium x *microdon* (T. Moore) Lovis & Vida [*A. obovatum* subsp. *lanceolatum* x *scolopendrium*]
Asplenium x *murbeckii* Dörfl. [*A. ruta-muraria* x *A. septentrionale*]
Asplenium x *alternifolium* Wulfen [*A. septentrionale* x *A. trichomanes* subsp. *trichomanes*]
Asplenium x *clermontae* Syme [*A. ruta-muraria* x *A. trichomanes* subsp. *quadrivalens*]

FAMILY Woodsiacea

Athyrium distentifolium Tausch ex Opiz **Alpine lady fem**
Athyrium distentifolium var. *flexile* (Newman) Jermy **Flexile lady fern**
Athyrium filix-femina (L.) Roth **Lady fern**
Gymnocarpium dryopteris (L.) Newman **Oak fern**
Gymnocarpium robertianum (Hoffm.) Newman **Limestone oak fern**
Cystopteris diaphana (Bory) Blasdell **Diaphanous bladder fern**
Cystopteris fragilis (L.) Bernh. **Brittle bladder fern**
Cystopteris fragilis dickeana R. Sim **Dickie's bladder fern**
Cystopteris montana (Lam.) Desv. **Mountain bladder fern**
Woodsia alpina (Bolton) Gray **Alpine woodsia**
Woodsia ilvensis (L.) R. Br. **Oblong woodsia**

FAMILY Dryopteridaceae

Polystichum aculeatum (L.) Roth **Hard shield fern**
Polystichum lonchitis (L.) Roth **Holly fern**
Polystichum setiferum (Forssk.) Woyn. **Soft shield fern**
Dryopteris aemula (Aiton) Kuntze **Hay-scented buckler fern**
Dryopteris affinis (E.J. Lowe) Fraser-Jenk. **Golden** or **scaly male fern**
Dryopteris borreri (Newman) Fraser-Jenk. **Borrer's scaly male fern**
Dryopteris cambrensis Fraser-Jenk. **Narrow scaly male fern**
Dryopteris carthusiana (Vill.) H.P. Fuchs **Narrow buckler fern**
Dryopteris cristata (L.) A. Gray **Crested** or **fen buckler fern**
Dryopteris dilatata (Hoffm.) A. Gray **Broad buckler fern**
Dryopteris expansa (C. Presl.) Fraser-Jenk. & Jermy **Northern buckler fern**
Dryopteris filix-mas (L.) Schott **Common male fern**
Dryopteris oreades Fomin **Mountain male fern**
Dryopteris submontana (Fraser-Jenk. & Jermy) Fraser-Jenk. **Rigid buckler fern**

HYBRIDS

Polystichum x *lonchitiforme* (Halácsy) Bech. [*P. lonchitis* x *P. setiferum*]
Polystichum x *illyricum* (Borbás) Hahne [*P. lonchitis* x *P. aculeatum*]
Polystichum x *bicknellii* (Christ) Hahne [*P. aculeatum* x *P. setiferum*]
Dryopteris x *mantoniae* Fraser-Jenk. & Corley [*D. filix-mas* x *D. oreades*]
Dryopteris x *pseudoabbreviata* Jermy [*D. aemula* x *D. oreades*]
Dryopteris x *uliginosa* (A. Braun ex Dôll) Kuntze ex Druce [*D. carthusiana* x *D. cristata*]
Dryopteris x *deweveri* (J.T. Jansen) J.T. Jansen & Wachter [*D. carthusiana* x *D. dilatata*]
Dryopteris x *sarvelae* Fraser-Jenk. & Jermy [*D. carthusiana* x *D. expansa*]
Dryopteris x *ambroseae* Fraser-Jenk. & Jermy [*D. dilatata* x *D. expansa*]
Dryopteris x *complexa* Fraser-Jenk. [*D. affinis* x *D. filix-mas*]
Dryopteris x *brathaica* Fraser-Jenk. & Reichst. [*D. carthusiana* x *D. filix-mas*]

FAMILY Blechnaceae

Blechnum spicant (L.) Roth **Hard fern**

FAMILY Azollaceae

Azolla filiculoides Lam. **American water fern**

Glossary of Pteridological terms

Some terms are used to describe features in one or more of the groups. These are coded as follows: C = clubmosses, Q = quillworts, H = horsetails, F = ferns, All = all groups

ANNULUS (pl. annuli) F: Specialised cells of sporangium opening mechanism [Latin: ring]. Used in the separation of Polypodium species (page 51). The annulus of a young sporangium is clearly seen as a brown line in two of the three Polypodium species

ANTHERIDIUM (pl. antheridia) All: Male organ on lower surface of prothallus [Greek: minute flower]

ARCHEGONIUM (pl. archegonia) All: Female organ on lower surface of prothallus [Greek: minute first one]

BIPINNATE F: Frond divided twice (see overleaf and page 40)

BLADE F: That portion of the leaf that has the pinnae, not including the stipe

BULBIL C: Detachable organs of vegetative reproduction (see *Huperzia selago*, page 22)

CROZIER F: Uncurling, young leaf

FROND F: Leaf (blade + stipe)

GAMETOPHYTE All: Result of spore germination, the minute bearer of the pteridophyte sex organs = prothallus (see sporophyte) [Greek: husband or sex cell-bearing plant]

GEMMA (pl. gemmae) C: Bulbils for vegetative reproduction [Latin: bud]

GENUS All: A group of species with common characteristics (see species) [Latin: with kin]

GLAND F: Organ of secretion, often on tip of microscopic hair

HETEROSPOROUS All: Spores and sporangia of two types: male and female – only *Selaginella, Isoetes, Azolla,* and *Pilularia*

HOMOSPOROUS All: Spores and sporangia of one type: hermaphrodite – all except *Selaginella, Isoetes, Azolla,* and *Pilularia*

HYBRID All: Offspring of two different species [Latin: mongrel]

INDUSIUM (pl. indusia) F: Protective membrane (if present) covering the sporangia in a sorus. Indusium shape is characteristic of and a diagnostic feature for each genus [Latin: clothing]

INFLEXED F: Turned or bent inwards as in the lowest pinnae of *Phegopteris connectilis*

INTERNODE F: Stem section between two nodes

LANCEOLATE F: Long, narrow, broadest at mid point [Latin: lance-shaped]

LEAF All: Frond

LIGULE Q and C: Small scale on leaf surface (*Selaginella* and *Isoetes*) [Latin: little tongue]

MEGASPORE C, Q, F: In heterosporous species: female spores [Greek: great spore]

MICROSPORE C, Q, F: In heterosporous species: male spores [Greek: small spore]

MIDRIB F: Distinct central vein in frond

NODE H: Stem joint [Latin: knot]

OBLONG F: Longer than broad, with more or less parallel sides

OVATE F: Broadest at mid-point and broader at base than at tip [Latin: egg-shaped]

OVATE-LANCEOLATE F: Broadly lanceolate or narrowly ovate

PARAPHYSIS (pl. paraphyses) F: sterile hairs (amidst sporangia of *Polypodium cambricum*) [Greek: side growth]

PINNA (pl pinnae) F: First division of a divided (pinnate) frond [Latin: feather, wing, fin]

PINNATE F: Frond divided once (see overleaf and page 40)

PINNULE F: Second division of a divided frond, division of a pinna

PINNULET F: Third division of a divided frond, division of a pinnule

PROTHALLUS All: Result of spore germination, the minute bearer of the pteridophyte sex organs = gamet-ophyte (see sporophyte) [Greek: first plant body]

RACHIS F: Blade mid-rib, excluding stipe [Latin: spine]

RHIZOME All: Creeping or contracted stem from which leaves and roots arise [Greek: cause to take root]

SCALE F: Pale to dark brown tissue paper-like appendage on rhizome or rachis

SIMPLY PINNATE F: Frond blade divided once

SORUS (pl. sori) F: A cluster of sporangia, usually protected by an indusium [Greek: heap]

SPECIES All: A group of organisms generally resembling each other and potentially capable of reproduction – second part of scientific name (see genus) [Latin: kind, sort, or variety]

SPORANGIUM (pl. sporangia) F: Spore capsule. Individual sporangia are more-or-less microscopic; their presence without a lens recognised as sori [Greek: spore vessel]

SPORE All: Microscopic dispersal agent, produced within sporangia on the sporophyte, giving rise to gametophyte and sex organs on germination [Greek: a sowing]

SPOROCARP F: Pod containing the sporangia (*Pilularia* only) [Greek: spore fruit]

SPOROPHYLL All: Frond which bears sporangia [Greek: spore leaf]

SPOROPHYTE All: The dominant pteridophyte plant: the clubmoss, quillwort, horsetail or fern plant identified in this guide, the producer of spores (see gametophyte & prothallus) [Greek: spore plant]

STIPE F: Leaf stalk, the non-leafy part of a frond [Latin: stalk]

STROBILUS C, H (pl. strobili): cone [Greek: twisted]

TRIPARTITE F: Frond divided into three distinct sections; eg. the frond of the fern (below)

TRIPINNATE F: Frond divided thrice (see below and page 40)

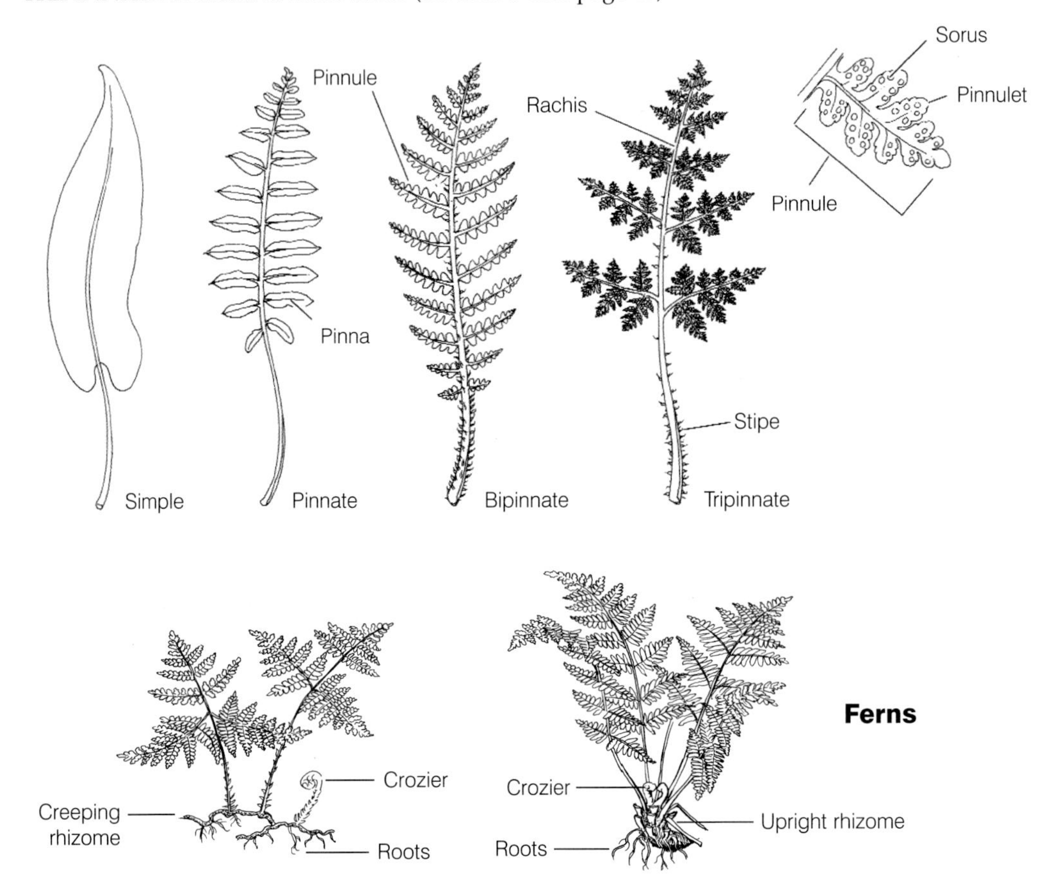

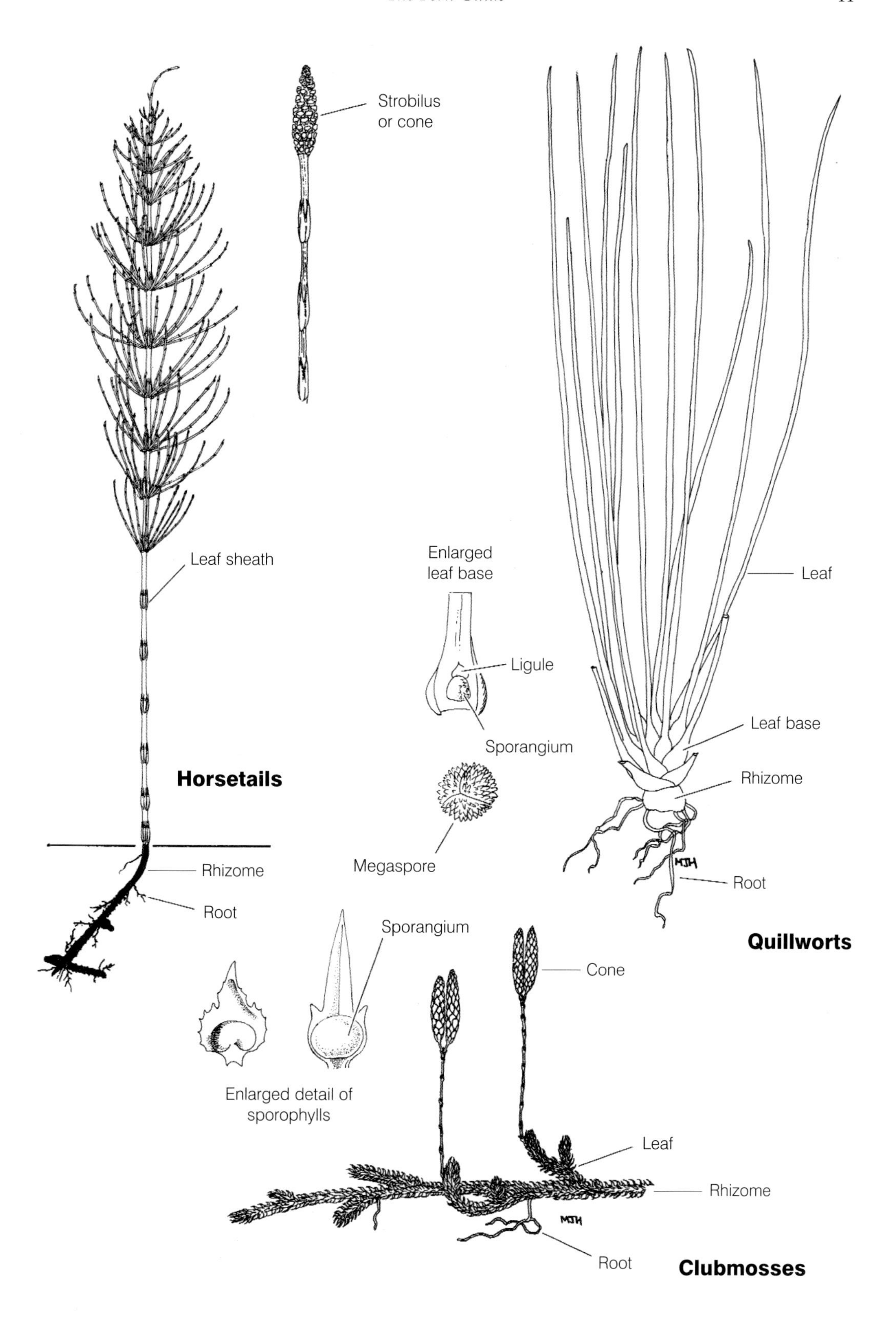
Strobilus
or cone
Leaf sheath
Horsetails
Rhizome
Root
Enlarged
leaf base
Ligule
Sporangium
Megaspore
Leaf
Leaf base
Rhizome
Root
Quillworts
Sporangium
Cone
Enlarged detail of
sporophylls
Leaf
Rhizome
Root
Clubmosses

ALIEN SPECIES

A number of foreign pteridophytes have joined the British flora, usually following escape from cultivation. The ornamental pond fern *Azolla filiculoides* is included in the key because it has escaped frequently in recent years (page 15). *Selaginella kraussiana* is a common glasshouse weed, sometimes successfully establishing itself out of doors in regions with a mild climate. South facing walls, especially behind warm kitchens and greenhouses, often support colonies of *Pteris cretica, P. vittata* or *Cyrtomium falcatum*, all grown commercially as houseplants. Other ferns which have escaped from gardens by spore, or in garden refuse, include: *Onoclea sensibilis, Matteuccia struthiopteris, Blechnum penna-marina* and *Polystichum acrostichoides*. These aliens are minor contributors to the British flora and will not be dealt with in detail by *The Fern Guide*. If they interest you, it is recommended that you refer to books on fern cultivation, for example Kaye (1968).

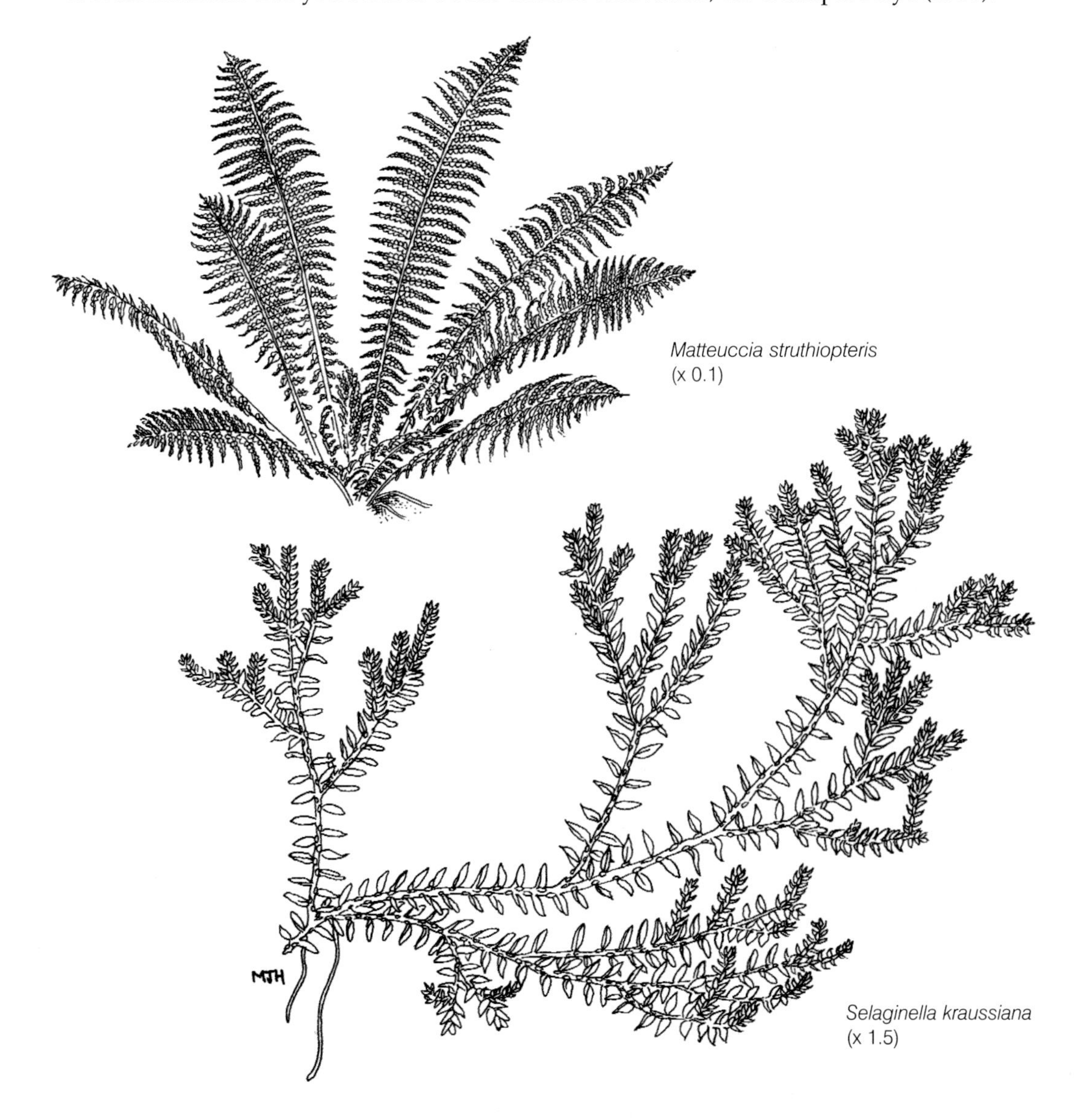

Matteuccia struthiopteris (x 0.1)

Selaginella kraussiana (x 1.5)

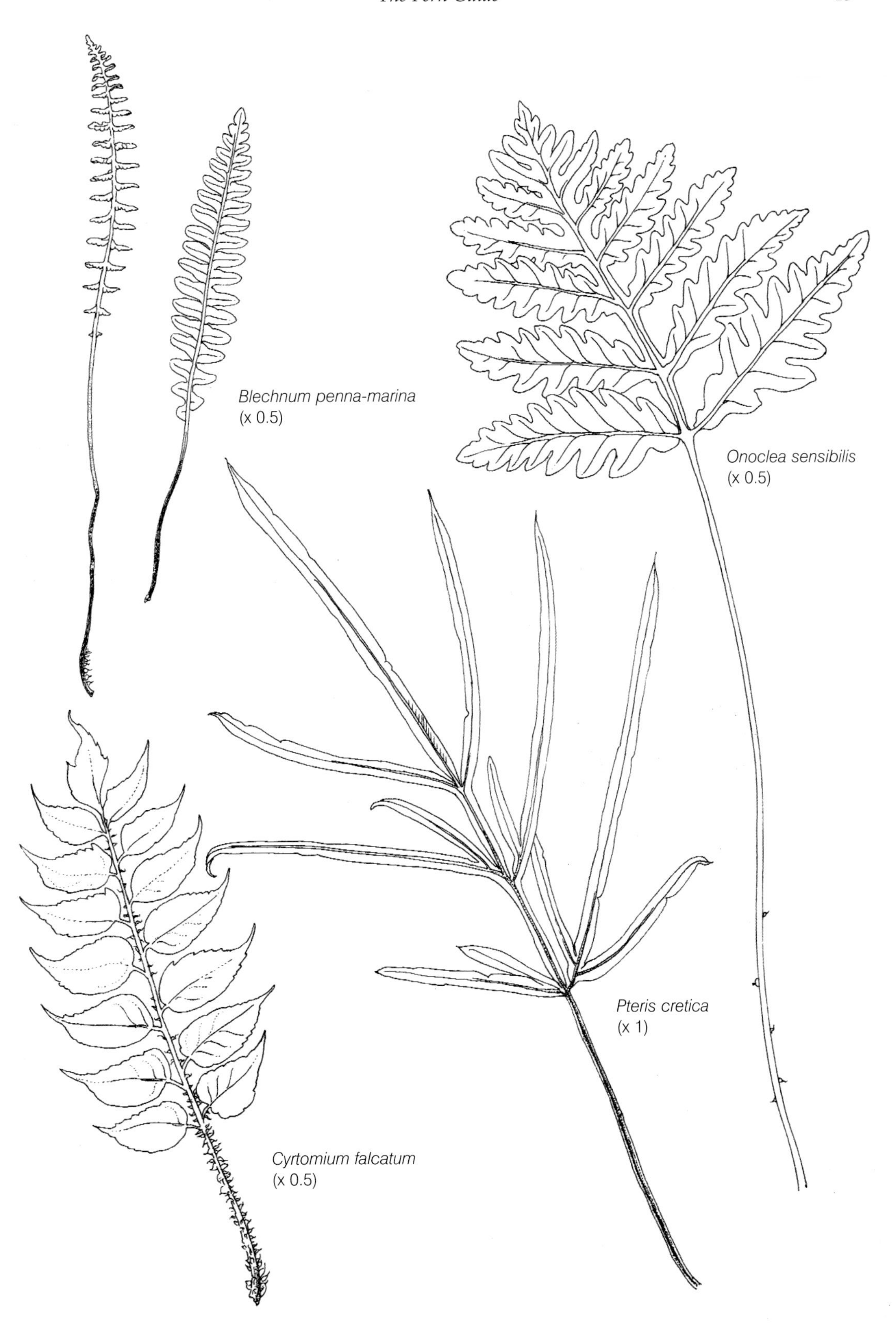
Blechnum penna-marina
(x 0.5)
Onoclea sensibilis
(x 0.5)
Pteris cretica
(x 1)
Cyrtomium falcatum
(x 0.5)

KEYS TO FERNS, CLUBMOSSES, QUILLWORTS AND HORSETAILS OF THE BRITISH ISLES

START HERE

1. Be as certain as you can that your unidentified specimen is not a juvenile or '*bonsai*' specimen (see page 3 *Select an adult fern*).

2. Starting at Key A: THE MAJOR GROUPS, compare your specimen with the paired descriptions that are labelled either with a location code e.g. **A1** or its alternative **or**.

3. Decide which description matches your specimen.

4. If the description matches a species on the present page, stop there.

5. If you do not have a match at this stage, move step by step through the keys as instructed by the 'Go to' directions (e.g. Go to G14, page 65), selecting from each pair of descriptions until you reach the page where your specimen is described.

6. If you reach a point where neither description matches your specimen backtrack by following the small location codes preceded by an arrow (e.g. **↑G9**) to the point where you think you went wrong and try again.

KEY A: THE MAJOR GROUPS

Key A starts by considering two fern species which are so different from any other British pteridophytes that they are excluded from the keys. Both are rare and they are so un-fern like that you are unlikely to think of them as ferns until you already know them. If your specimen does not fit either of these two descriptions, go to A3 and continue through the key till you have identified the major group your specimen is from. You will then be directed to the relevant key for that group.

A1 A floating aquatic plant. Its tiny, overlapping inflated leaves alternate along stems which they hide. The leaves are light green, often flushed bright pink, sometimes with a mealy appearance.

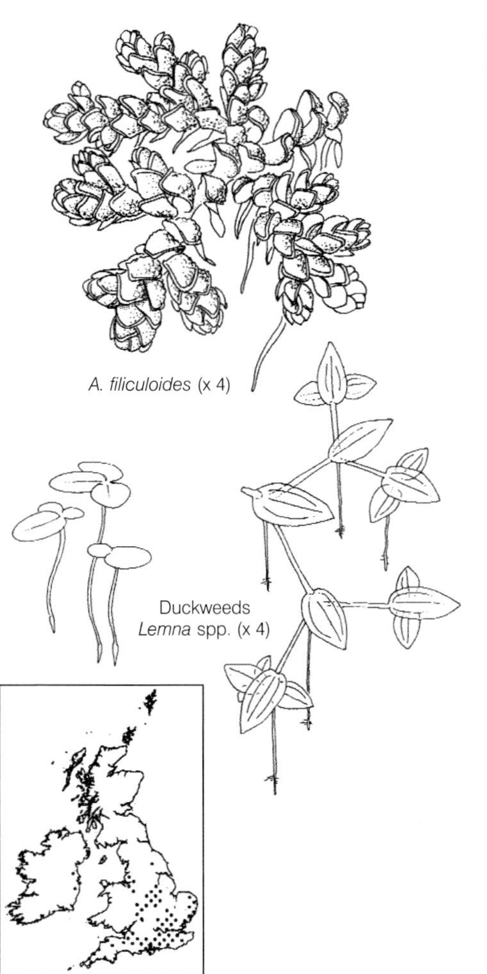

An aquatic originally introduced from North America which floats on the water surface of an increasing number of lakes, ponds, canals and slow rivers, mainly in the south of England. Its mealy appearance is due to a liberal coating of waxy particles which, along with leaf air bladders, make the plant unsinkable and astonishingly unwettable. Prod it under the water and it bobs up again enthusiastically.

If you do find this fern by accident you will have probably happened upon a slow-flowing river or lake with a dense summer bloom of *Azolla*, an incredible blanket of brownish-pink where you would expect to see water. This species may well be responding to pollution reduction! Some rivers have been improved and the water surface, once covered with duckweed which thrives on the high nitrogen supply in semi-polluted waterways, gives way to *Azolla*. The water fern succeeds because it has its own symbiotic cyanobacteria from which it obtains nutrients manufactured from atmospheric nitrogen. In a few places this unusual fern has become a pest. You are unlikely to confuse this fern with the duckweeds which also inhabit the water surface, for *Azolla* is more leafy, cushion-like, waxy and often tinged with pink.

American water fern *Azolla filiculoides*

or If not the American water fern, *Azolla filiculoides*, go to A2, overleaf →

A2
↑A1

At a distance, a grass-like plant growing in dense green swards. On closer examination, the "leaves" are cylindrical and emerge, uncoiling in a very fern-like manner, from a creeping rhizome which frequently bears its little propagules (sporocarps) the "pills" after which it is named.

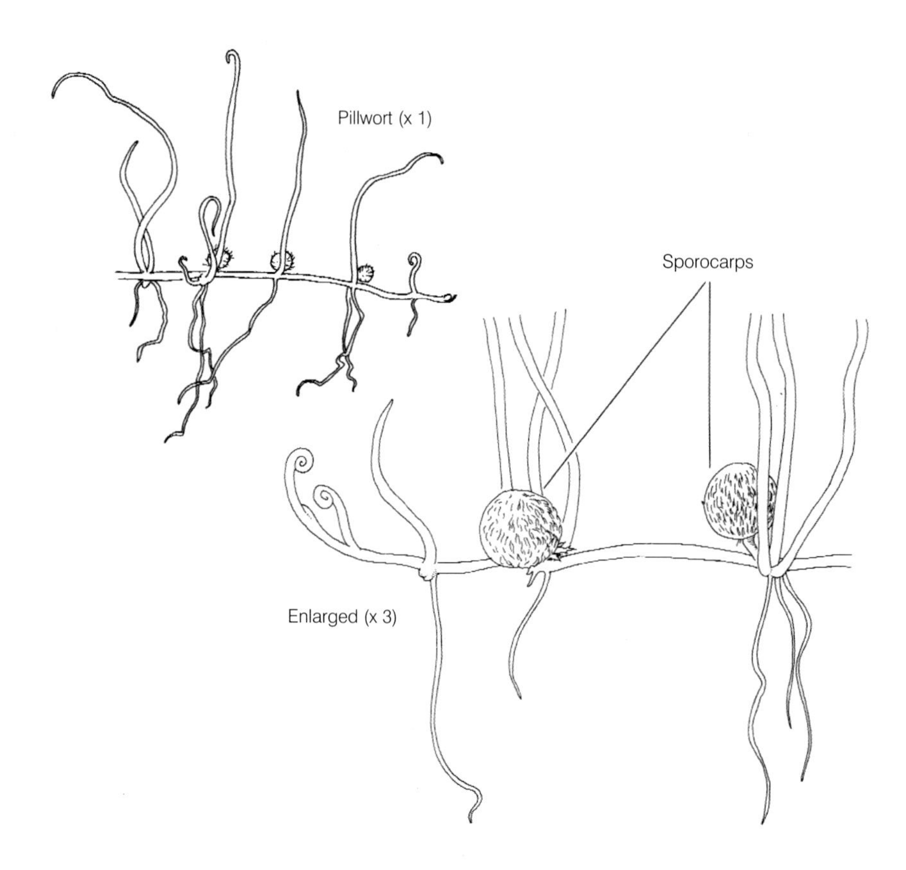

This second oddity is the pillwort, *Pilularia globulifera*, an increasingly rare native fern. It inhabits pond margins which are inundated during most of the year, but which partially, but not totally dry up in the summer. Such ideal conditions are unusual and disappearing.

Pillwort *Pilularia globulifera*

or If not the pillwort, go to A3, opposite ----→

A3 **↑A2** Creeping or stiffly tufted plant with minute simple leaves (less than 5mm long) clothing both rhizome and shoots with pale to bright yellow sporangia in leaf angles of upper parts of shoots or in terminal cones.

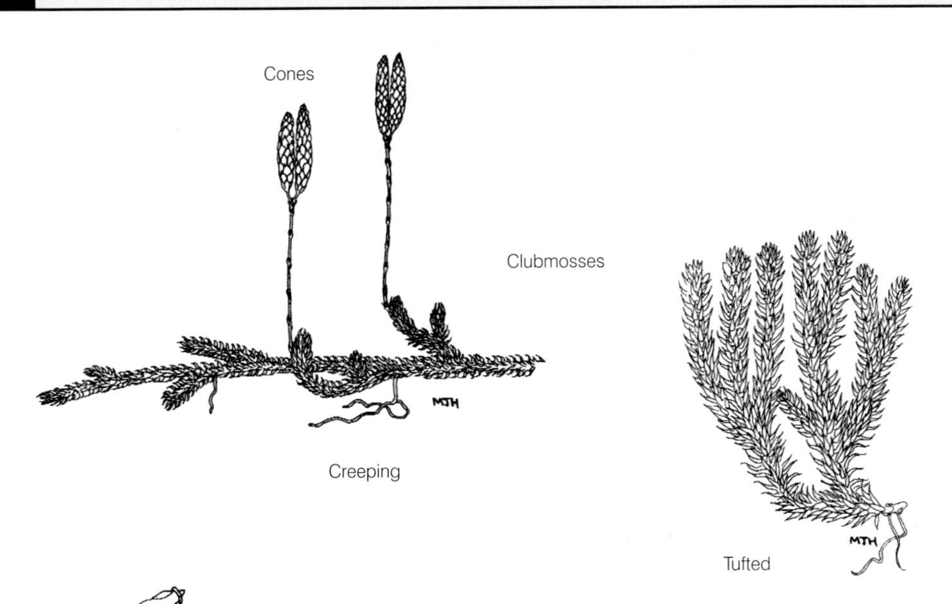

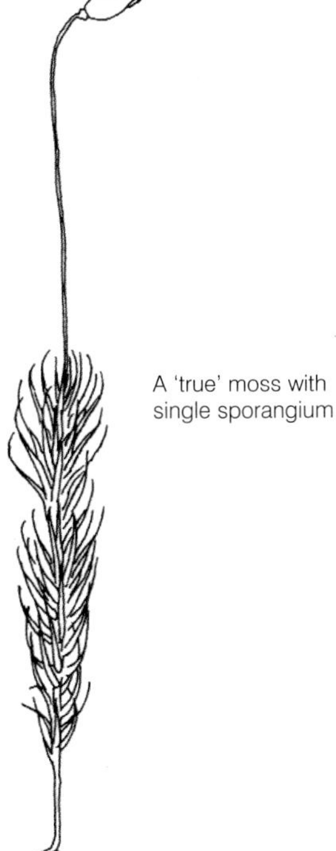

Do not be misled by the term 'clubmoss'. These pteridophytes are called clubmosses because their appearance is superficially moss-like, but they must not be confused with the true mosses which, if they have the creeping habit, remain horizontal and, if tufted, do not have a creeping rhizome. Spore production is very different, the moss sporangium being borne singly, usually at the tip of a long thin stalk (see illustration left). Lycopod sporangia are borne numerously in single or paired cones. Each sporangium in a cone sits on a small leaf known as a sporophyll. Because they have vascular tissue and a thick leaf cuticle, the clubmosses may feel stiff to the touch whereas mosses tend to be soft.

Clubmoss families
Lycopodiaceae and *Selaginellaceae*

Go to KEY B page 21 ---------→

or If not a clubmoss, go to A4, overleaf ---------→

A4
↑A3

Small (no more than 15-25 cm high), rush-like, aquatic or semi aquatic plant. The leaves are cylindrical with concave inner faces and broad sheathing bases that enclose the sporangia, which appear granular.

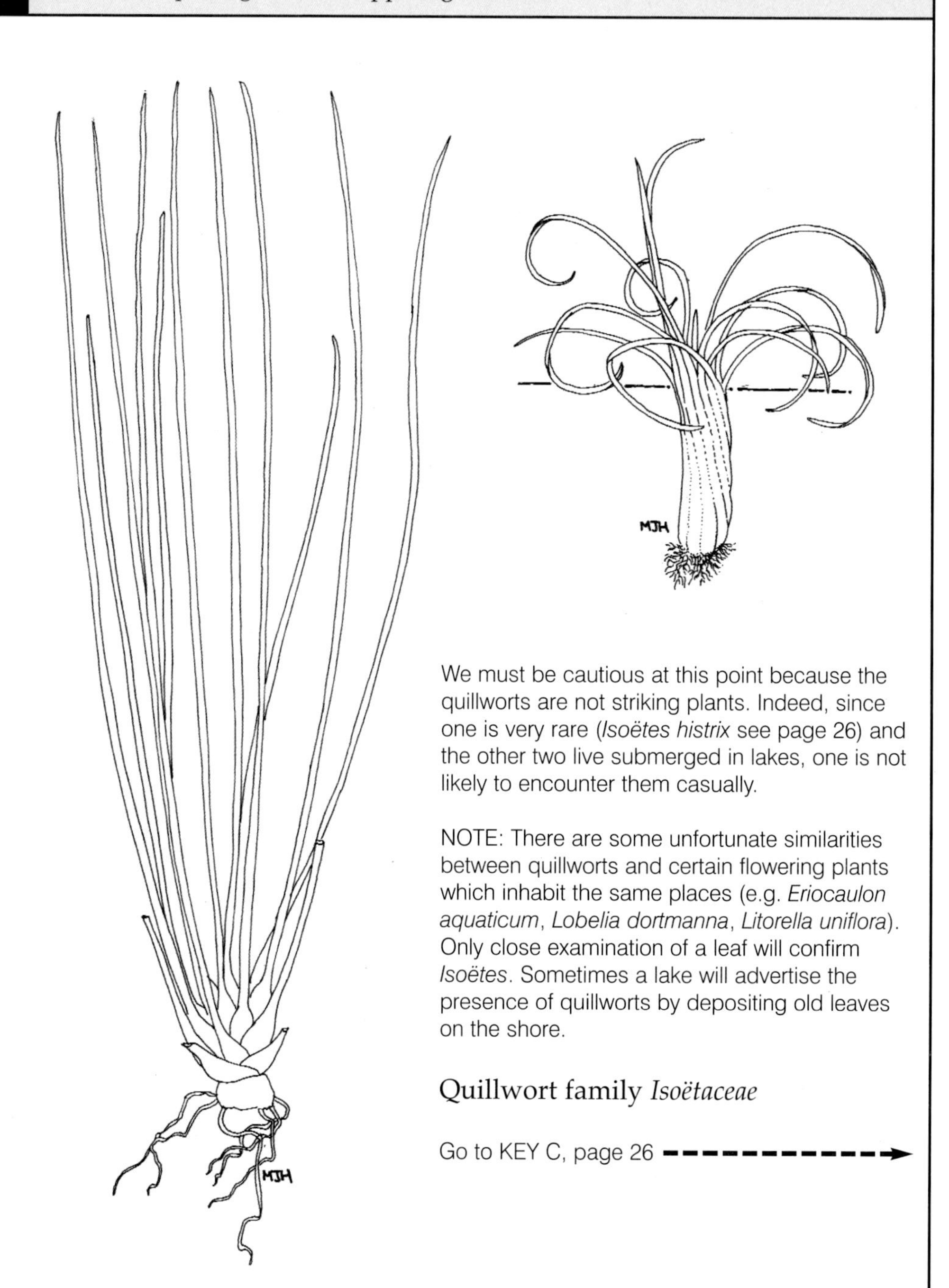

We must be cautious at this point because the quillworts are not striking plants. Indeed, since one is very rare (*Isoëtes histrix* see page 26) and the other two live submerged in lakes, one is not likely to encounter them casually.

NOTE: There are some unfortunate similarities between quillworts and certain flowering plants which inhabit the same places (e.g. *Eriocaulon aquaticum*, *Lobelia dortmanna*, *Litorella uniflora*). Only close examination of a leaf will confirm *Isoëtes*. Sometimes a lake will advertise the presence of quillworts by depositing old leaves on the shore.

Quillwort family *Isoëtaceae*

Go to KEY C, page 26 ------------→

or If not a quillwort, go to A5, opposite ------------→

A5
↑A4

Shoots have jointed stems which could easily be pulled into sections (please avoid being destructive) and each joint bears a whorl of scale leaves and, sometimes, branches.

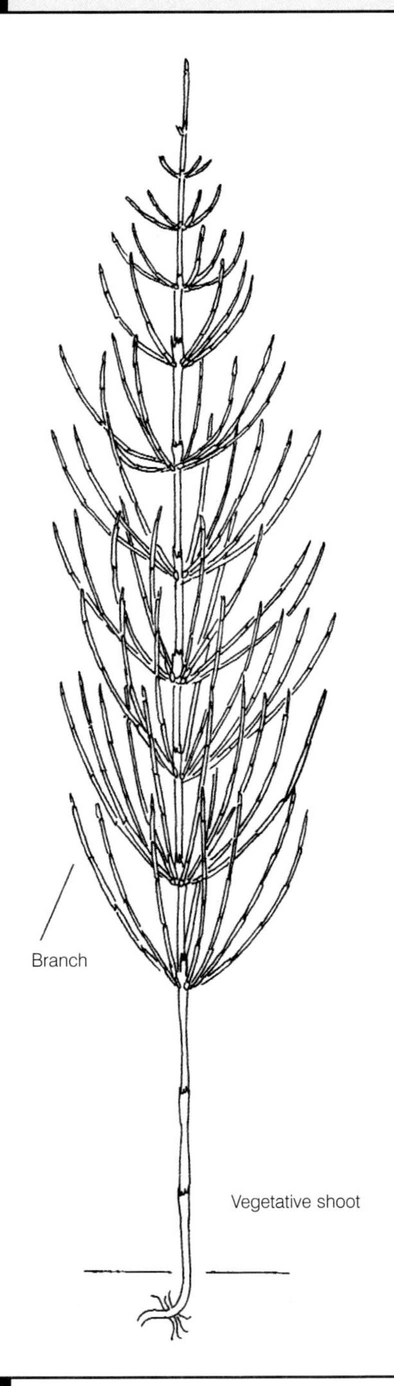

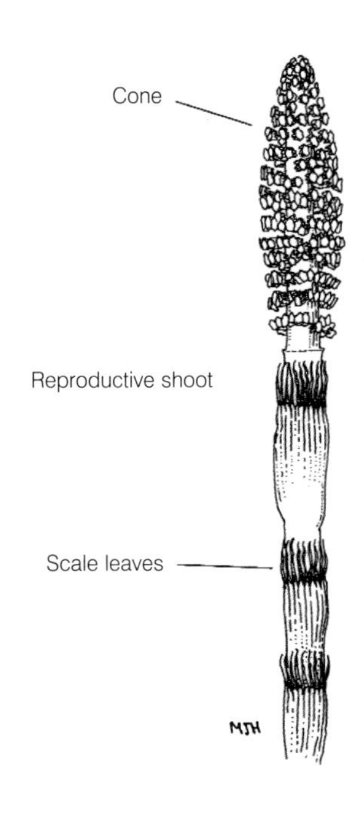

NOTE: there is but one British plant with which to confuse horsetails. Mare's tail, (*Hippuris vulgaris*) which grows in open water, is an angiosperm with, very inconspicuous, flowers. Its whorled leaves are flat and leaf-like, quite unlike the side branches of *Equisetum* species whose jointed stems and branches set them apart. Gardeners who curse the weed 'mare's tail' are mistaken – they mean the field horsetail *Equisetum arvense*.

Horsetail, family *Equisetaceae*

Go to Key D page 28 ➔

or If not a horsetail, go to A6, overleaf ➔

A6
↑A5

If the leaves are like one of those illustrated below it is (hopefully) a fern, a member of one of many fern families (see checklist, page 5). Remember that adult ferns generally have sporangia which you may need to find to achieve identification. Note also the growth habit: the rhizome may either creep about, throwing up leaves at intervals, or may be contracted and vertical, clustering the leaves and giving the whole plant a tufted or shuttlecock-like form.

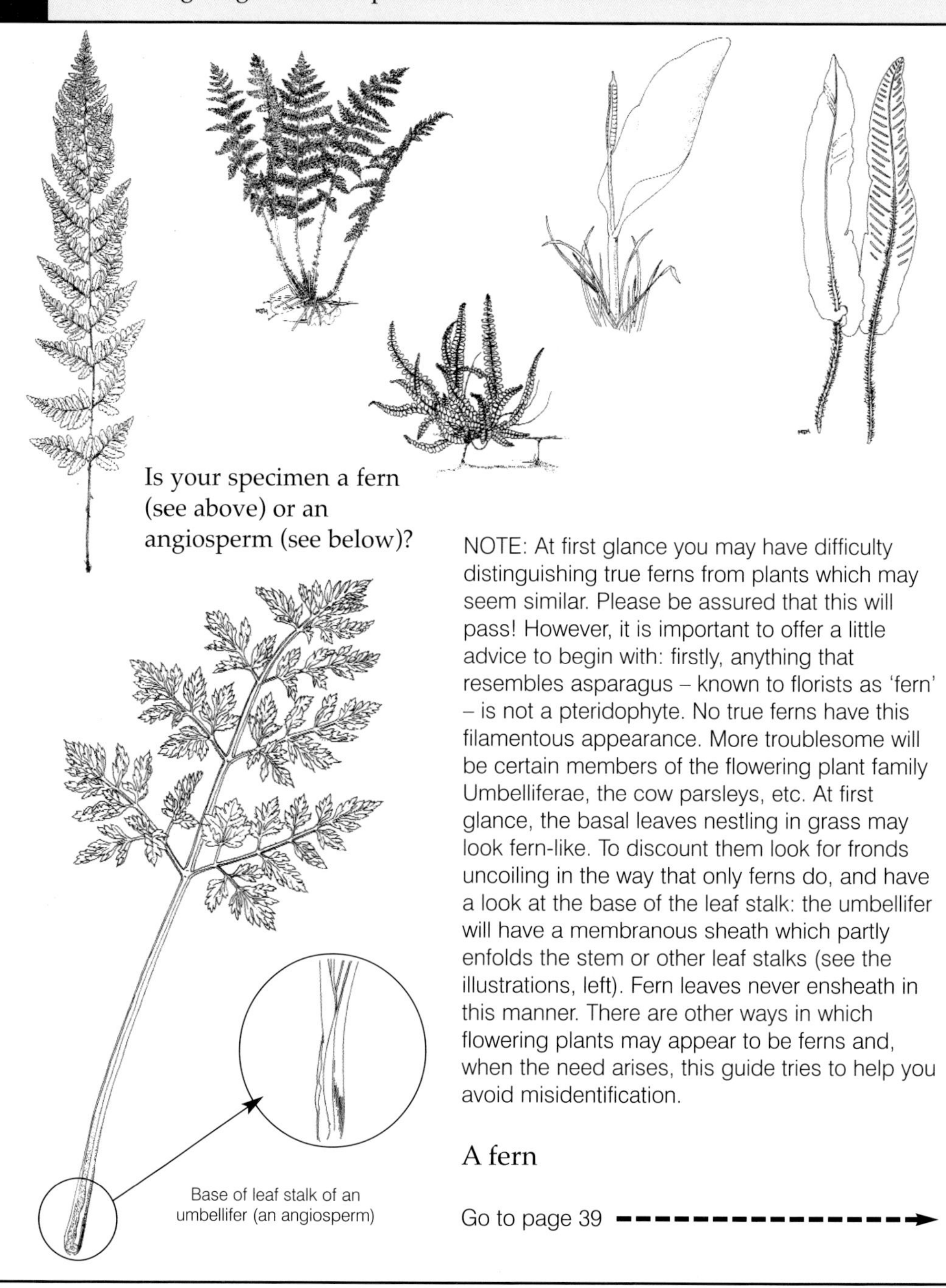

Is your specimen a fern (see above) or an angiosperm (see below)?

NOTE: At first glance you may have difficulty distinguishing true ferns from plants which may seem similar. Please be assured that this will pass! However, it is important to offer a little advice to begin with: firstly, anything that resembles asparagus – known to florists as 'fern' – is not a pteridophyte. No true ferns have this filamentous appearance. More troublesome will be certain members of the flowering plant family Umbelliferae, the cow parsleys, etc. At first glance, the basal leaves nestling in grass may look fern-like. To discount them look for fronds uncoiling in the way that only ferns do, and have a look at the base of the leaf stalk: the umbellifer will have a membranous sheath which partly enfolds the stem or other leaf stalks (see the illustrations, left). Fern leaves never ensheath in this manner. There are other ways in which flowering plants may appear to be ferns and, when the need arises, this guide tries to help you avoid misidentification.

Base of leaf stalk of an umbellifer (an angiosperm)

A fern

Go to page 39 ---------------→

KEY B: THE BRITISH CLUBMOSSES

B1 If the leaves are untoothed or only slightly serrated, and the sporangia, if present, are all of one type (globular but unlobed) it is a homosporous clubmoss of the family Lycopodiaceae.

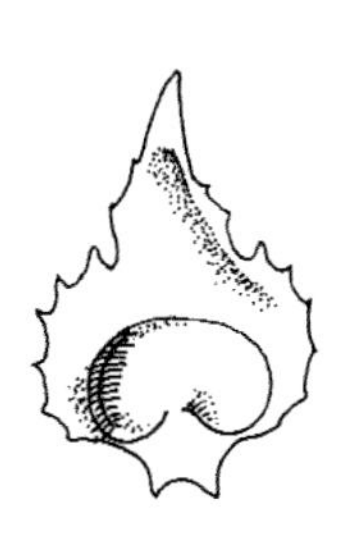

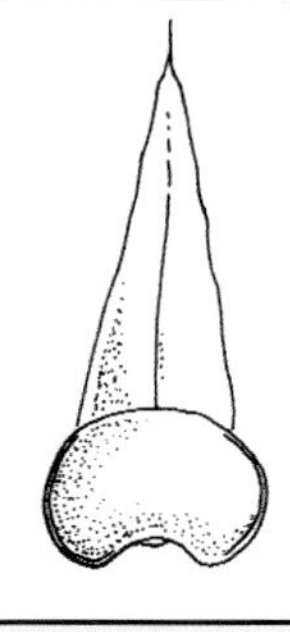

Go to B2, overleaf

or If the leaves are markedly toothed, particularly towards the base, and the sporangia, if present, are of two types – one simple, kidney-shaped and the other four-lobed – it is a heterosporous clubmoss or spikemoss of the family Selaginellaceae. This family is represented in Britain by the lesser clubmoss, a diminutive plant (3.5cm high), growing in moist calcareous or base-rich turf.

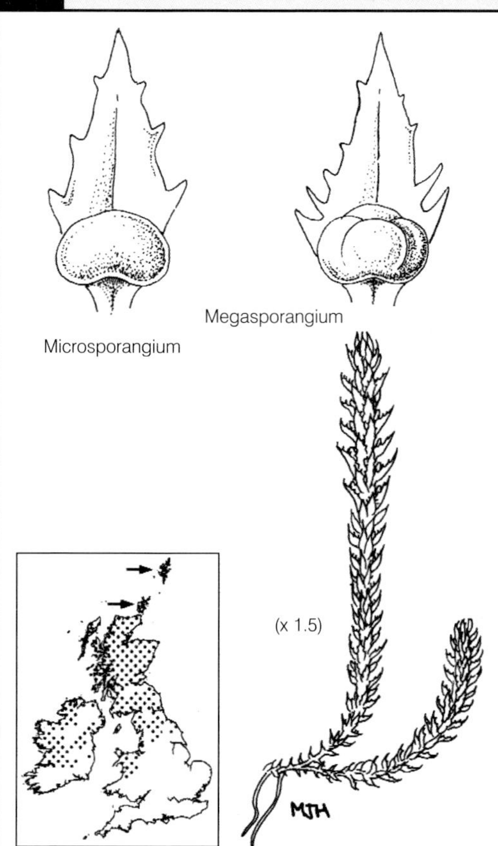

NOTE: *Selaginella selaginoides* is so small as to be easily overlooked. However, it is not uncommon and if you know where to look it is often possible to find it. It grows mainly in the mountains but may be found in calcareous maritime or limestone turf. In uplands, look for damp, nutrient rich flushes where the vegetation is richly diverse and lush.

You may well find the bright yellow-green shoots of *Selaginella* in crevices and on ledges where competition from other plants is not too great. Many mosses will be of similar stature but will not have the sporangia in cones.The moss sporangium is single, often borne on a long thin stalk and the leaf has no ligule (see page 17).

CONFIRMATION: carefully remove a single stem leaf and inspect the base of its inner face with a hand lens. The leaf of *Selaginella* has a tiny lobe known as a ligule. The ligule is absent from the leaves of all Lycopod species.

Lesser clubmoss *Selaginella selaginoides*

B2
↑B1

The stems arise, branching and spreading from a single point and bear green, heart-shaped bulbils towards their tips.

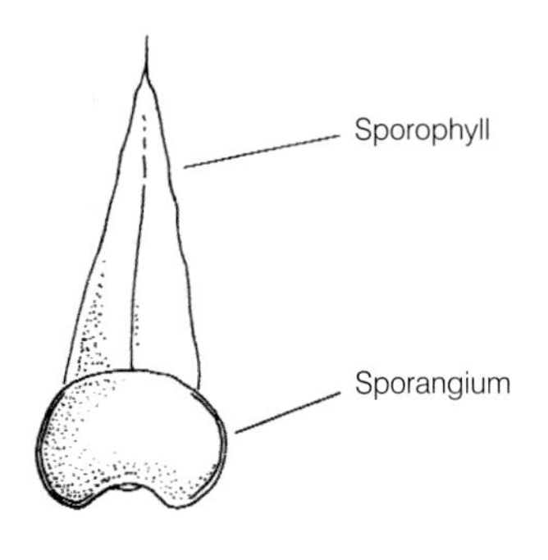

(x 1)

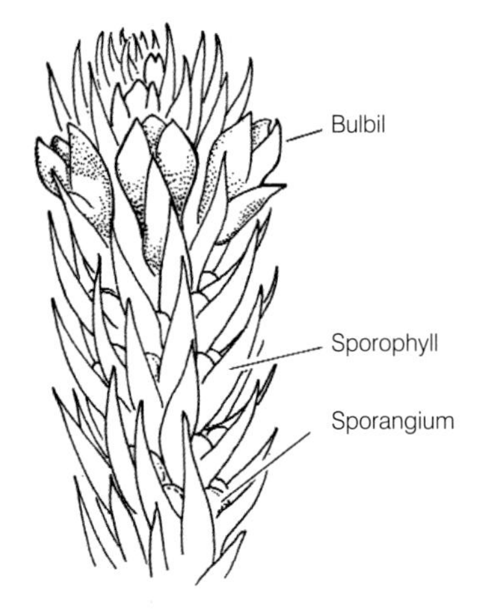

Common in alpine turf and on rocky mountain ledges.

Fir clubmoss *Huperzia selago*

or

The stems ascend from a creeping rhizome and have no bulbils (mountain or lowland species).

Go to B3, opposite ➞

B3
↑B2

The blue-green stem leaves are inserted on the stem in opposite pairs alternating at 90°, and the branches group to form untidy rosettes in mountain turf.

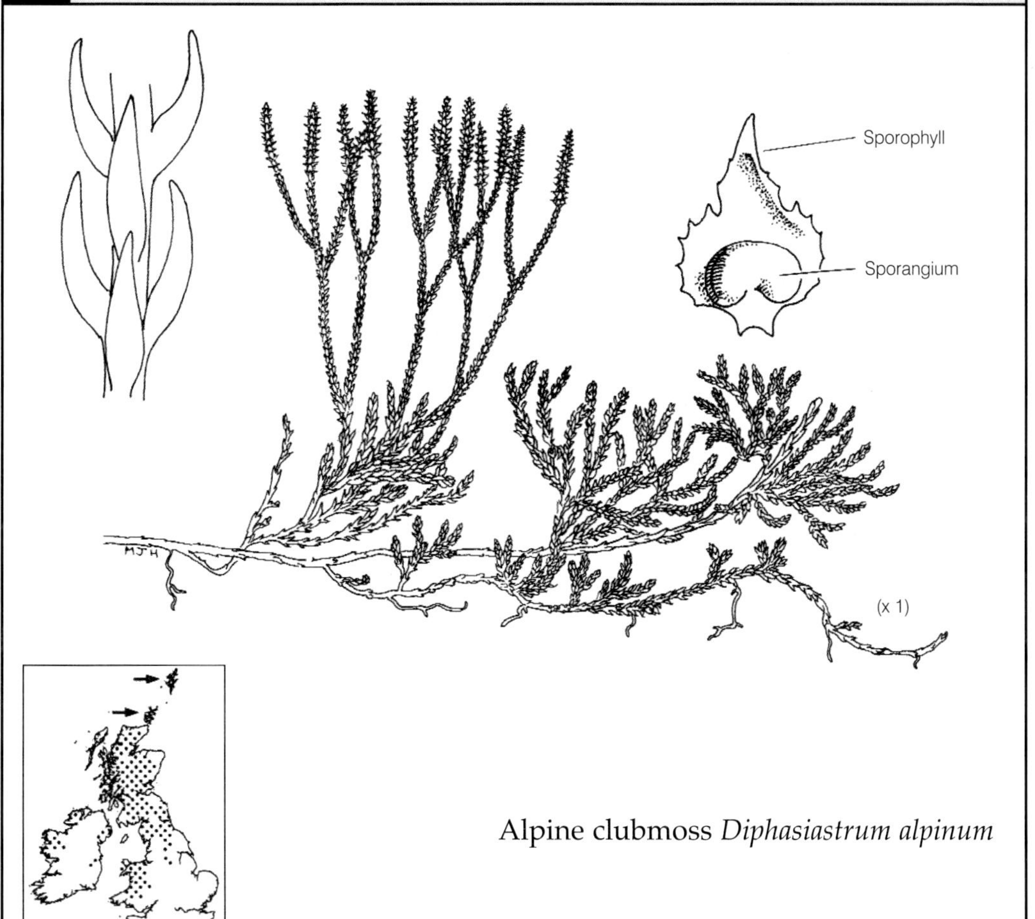

Alpine clubmoss *Diphasiastrum alpinum*

or

The stem leaves are inserted on the stem in a truly spiral pattern.

Stem leaves

Go to B4, overleaf →

B4
↑B3

The plant is very small, only 2-5(-10)cm tall growing on open, wet, acid peat in lowland regions.

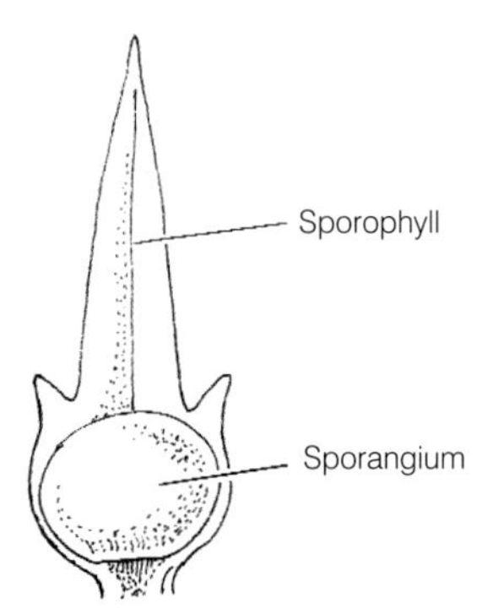

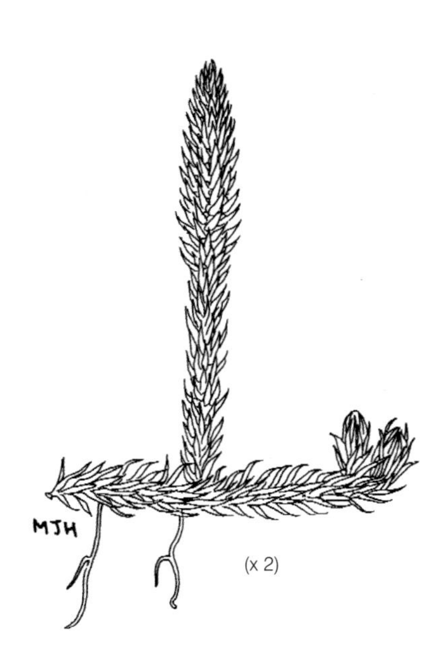

This species never forms dense patches because the stems die back in winter and only the terminal bud remains green ready for the new year's growth. Its cones, which are borne singly on short aerial stems, are bright green at first, turning to a dull yellow by mid-summer.

Marsh clubmoss *Lycopodiella inundata*

or

The plant is robust and 5-20cm tall, a wide-ranging creeper of mountains (rarely lowland).

Go to B5, opposite --→

B5
↑B4

Plant is robust and wide ranging with clusters of upright branches bearing single, unstalked cones. Silvery grey-green in appearance (due to hair tips on the crowded leaves).

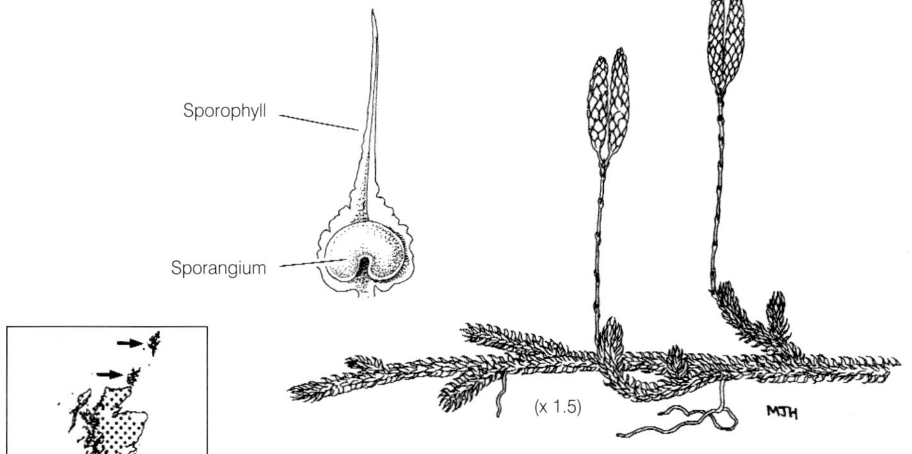

A species of mountain grassland and, increasingly rarely, in well-drained lowland situations. The leaves on the cone-bearing stalks are green, turning to a striking pale yellow by mid summer.

Stag's horn clubmoss *Lycopodium clavatum*

or

Plant is robust, with a wide-ranging rhizome from which branches arise in separate clusters, and bearing single, unstalked cones. Has bright green leaves without hair-points.

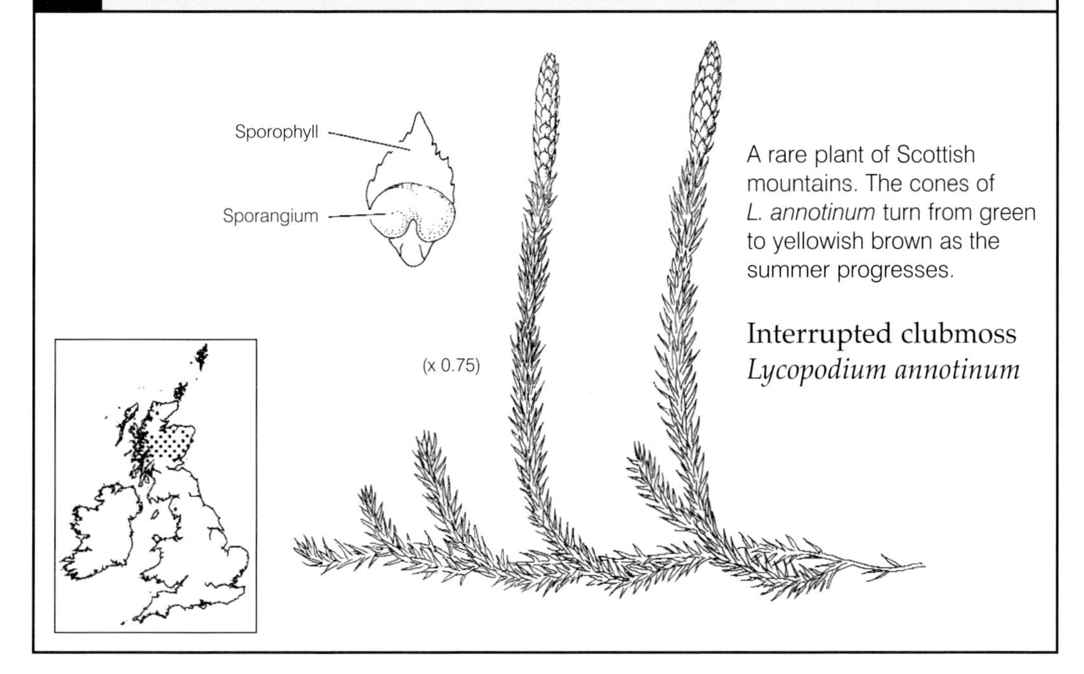

A rare plant of Scottish mountains. The cones of *L. annotinum* turn from green to yellowish brown as the summer progresses.

Interrupted clubmoss *Lycopodium annotinum*

KEY C: THE BRITISH QUILLWORTS

C1 Plant has curled leaves 3-8cm long, is terrestrial, growing in sandy hollows, submerged (if at all) only in winter (Cornwall, Alderney and Guernsey). Very rare.

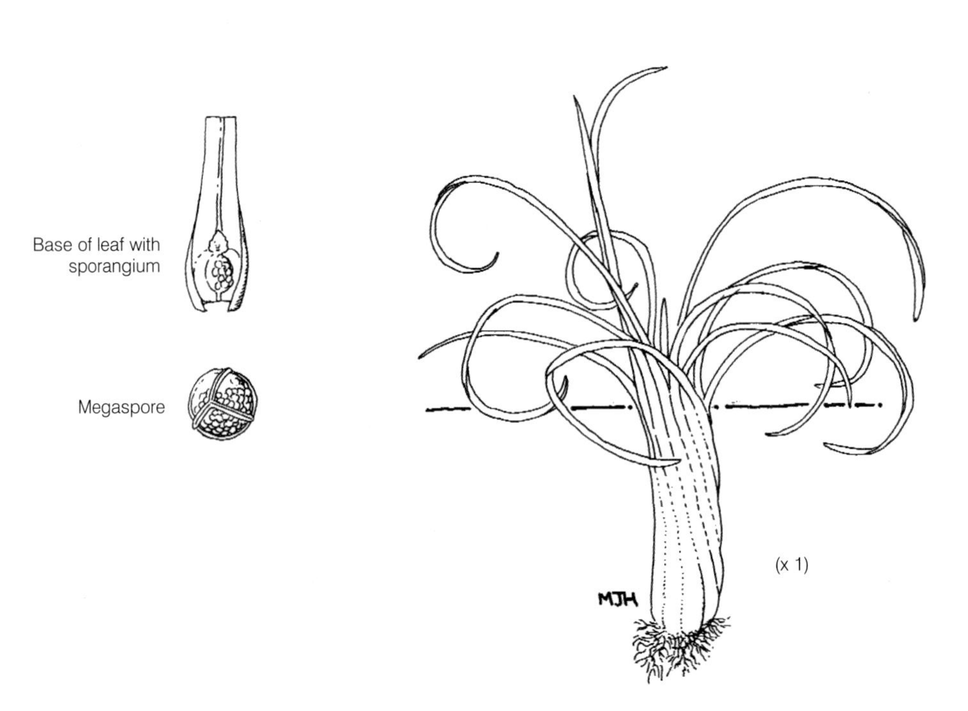

Land quillwort *Isoëtes histrix*

or Plant has straight leaves and is fully aquatic, growing in the clear water of lakes and upland tarns.

Go to C2, opposite ---------------------------------------→

Plant has soft, almost floppy leaves which are 5-25cm long, gradually tapering to the tip.

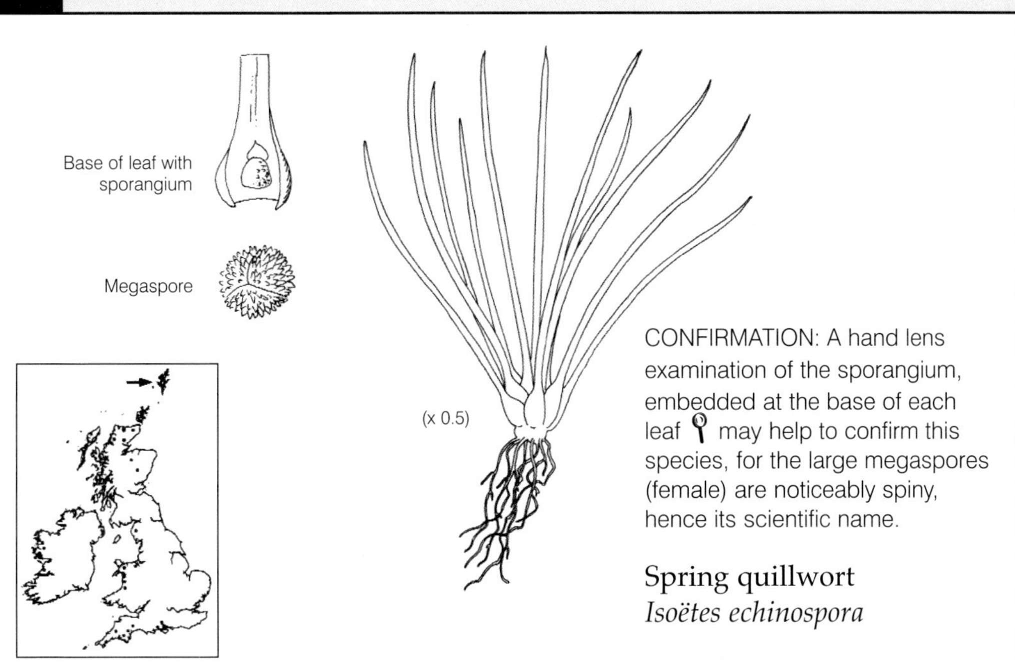

CONFIRMATION: A hand lens examination of the sporangium, embedded at the base of each leaf may help to confirm this species, for the large megaspores (female) are noticeably spiny, hence its scientific name.

Spring quillwort
Isoëtes echinospora

or Plant has stiff leaves which are 10-45cm long, parallel-sided, and abruptly tapered at the tip.

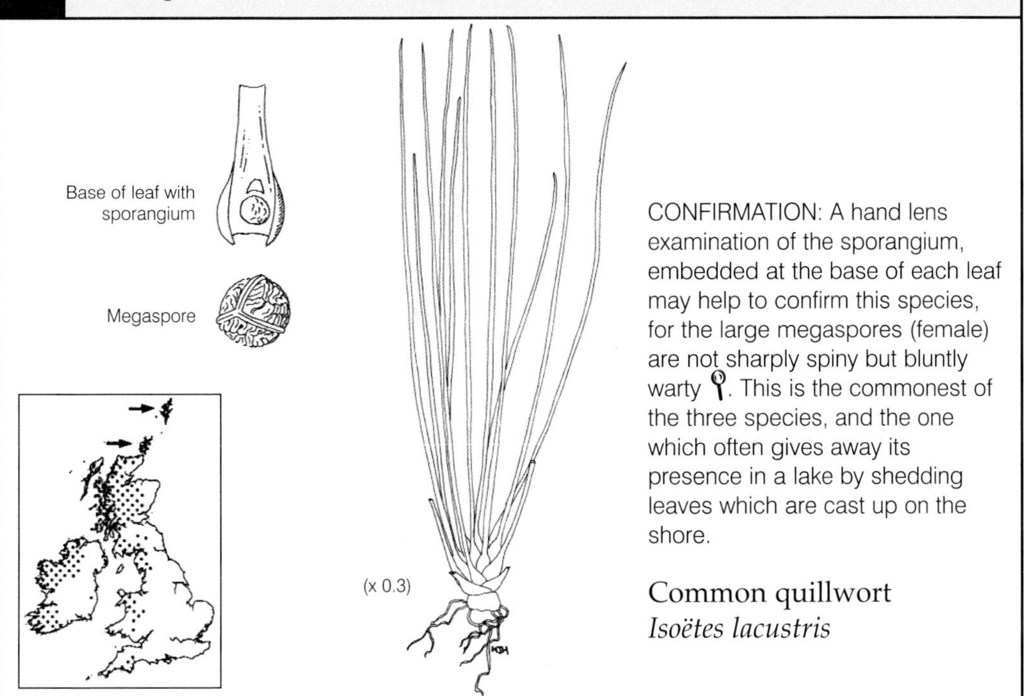

CONFIRMATION: A hand lens examination of the sporangium, embedded at the base of each leaf may help to confirm this species, for the large megaspores (female) are not sharply spiny but bluntly warty. This is the commonest of the three species, and the one which often gives away its presence in a lake by shedding leaves which are cast up on the shore.

Common quillwort
Isoëtes lacustris

KEY D: THE BRITISH HORSETAILS

D1 Plant found in March and April, with pale, almost white shoots bearing reproductive cones.

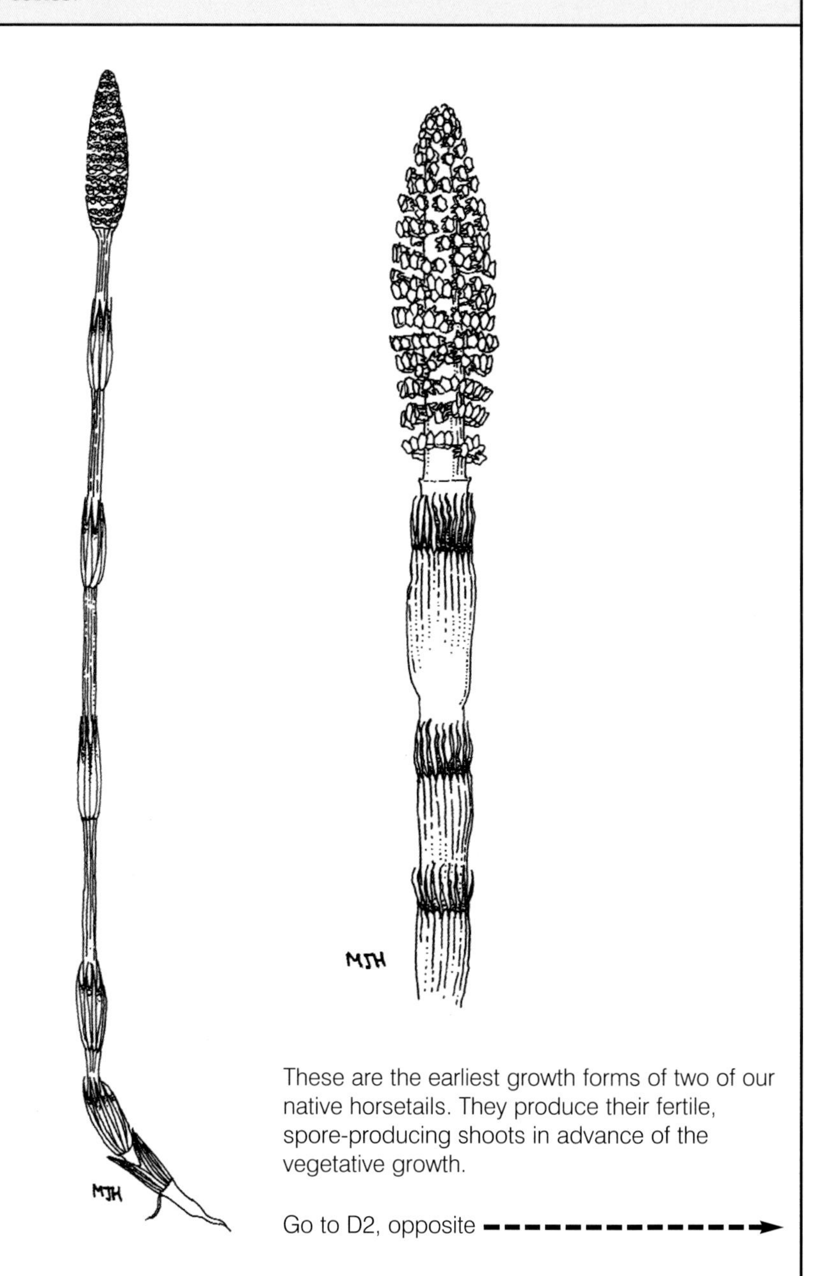

These are the earliest growth forms of two of our native horsetails. They produce their fertile, spore-producing shoots in advance of the vegetative growth.

Go to D2, opposite →

or Plant found from late April onwards, with green shoots.

Go to D3, page 30 →

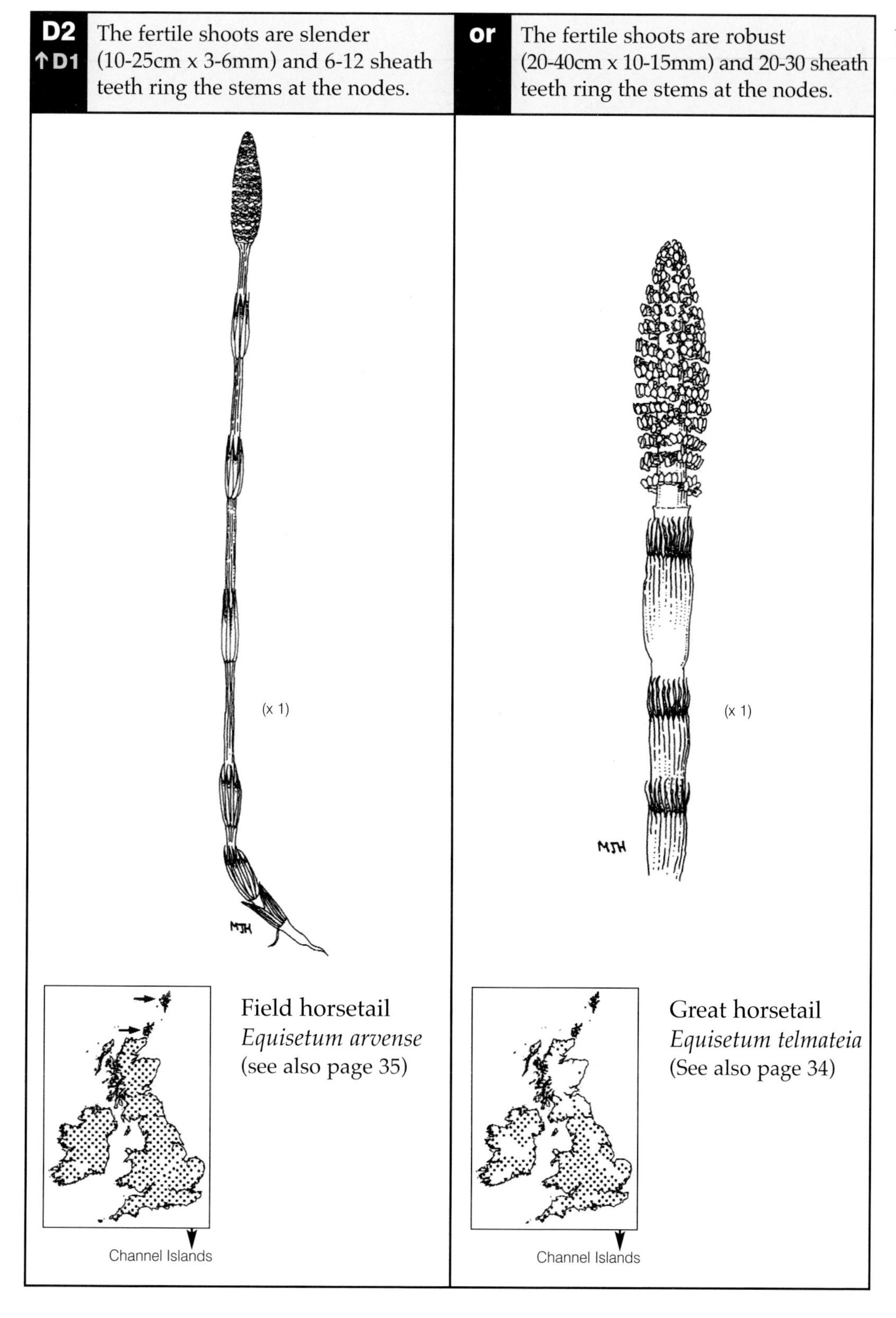
D2
↑D1
The fertile shoots are slender (10-25cm x 3-6mm) and 6-12 sheath teeth ring the stems at the nodes.
or
The fertile shoots are robust (20-40cm x 10-15mm) and 20-30 sheath teeth ring the stems at the nodes.
(x 1)
MJH
(x 1)
MJH
Field horsetail
Equisetum arvense
(see also page 35)
Channel Islands
Great horsetail
Equisetum telmateia
(See also page 34)
Channel Islands

D3 ↑D1 The green summer stems are unbranched or irregularly branched.

Go to D4, below

or The green summer stems have regular whorls of branches.

Go to D7, page 33

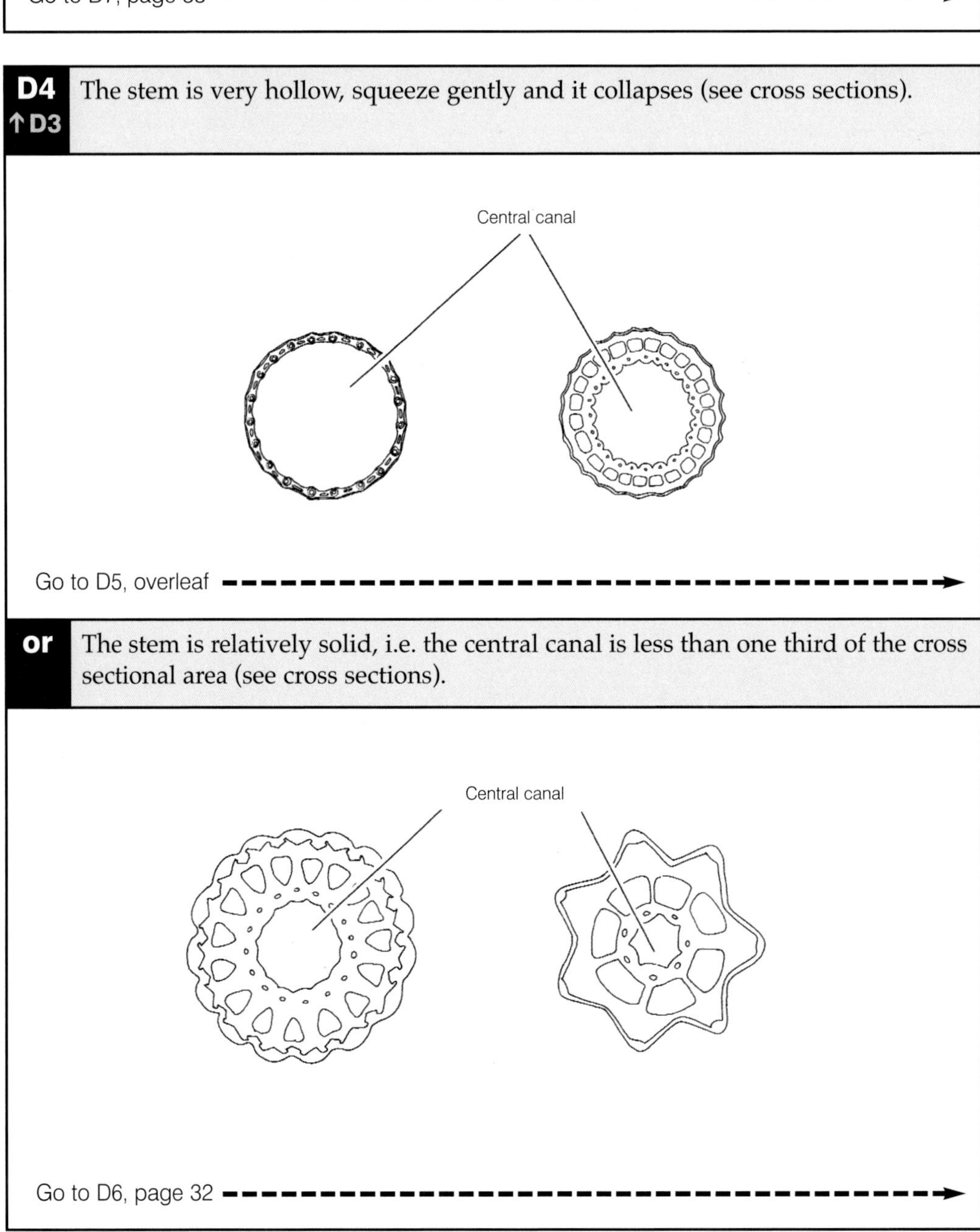

D4 ↑D3 The stem is very hollow, squeeze gently and it collapses (see cross sections).

Go to D5, overleaf

or The stem is relatively solid, i.e. the central canal is less than one third of the cross sectional area (see cross sections).

Go to D6, page 32

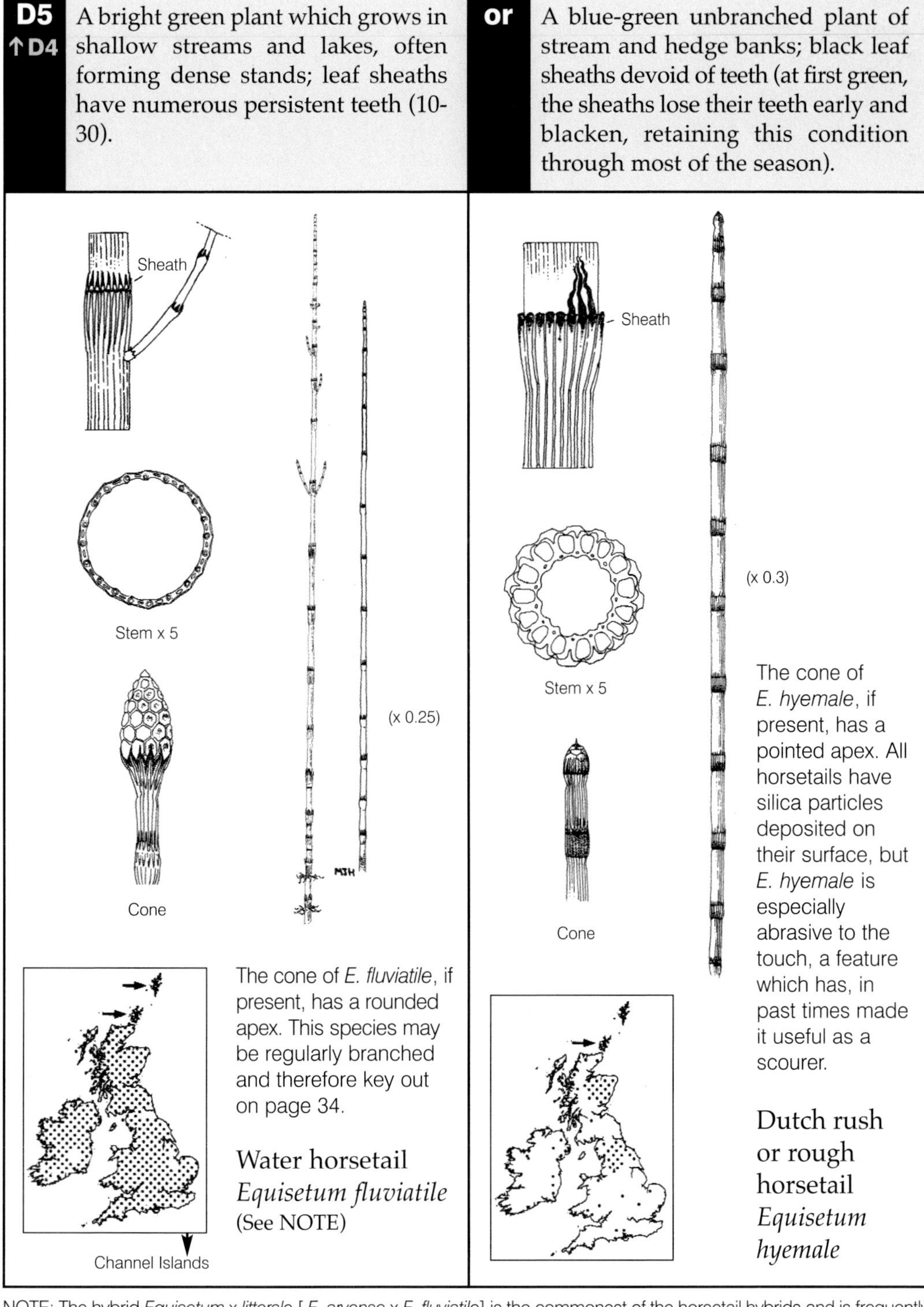

D5
↑D4

A bright green plant which grows in shallow streams and lakes, often forming dense stands; leaf sheaths have numerous persistent teeth (10-30).

The cone of *E. fluviatile*, if present, has a rounded apex. This species may be regularly branched and therefore key out on page 34.

Water horsetail
Equisetum fluviatile
(See NOTE)

or

A blue-green unbranched plant of stream and hedge banks; black leaf sheaths devoid of teeth (at first green, the sheaths lose their teeth early and blacken, retaining this condition through most of the season).

The cone of *E. hyemale*, if present, has a pointed apex. All horsetails have silica particles deposited on their surface, but *E. hyemale* is especially abrasive to the touch, a feature which has, in past times made it useful as a scourer.

Dutch rush or rough horsetail
Equisetum hyemale

NOTE: The hybrid *Equisetum* x *littorale* [*E. arvense* x *E. fluviatile*] is the commonest of the horsetail hybrids and is frequently encountered in the vicinity of its parents, generally, though not exclusively, in coastal situations. It is best described as a robust colony, the individuals of which resemble *E. arvense* with a long naked shoot apex. The stem canal is of intermediate diameter. The technique in Fig. 3 (p. 36) will help you to distinguish this hybrid from its two relatives.

D6
↑D4

A short, slender plant (20-50cm x 2-3mm), bearing dark leaf sheaths with white teeth.

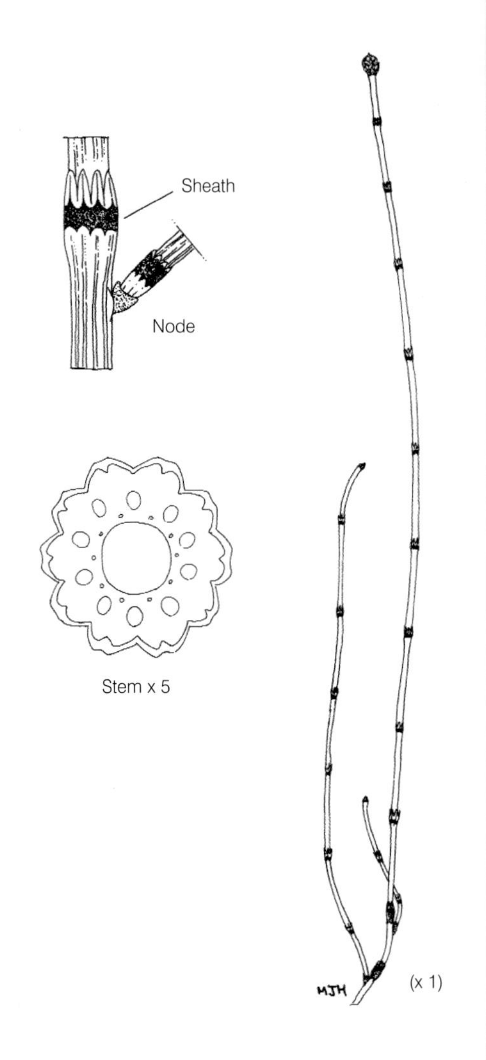

The cone of *E. variegatum*, if present, has a pointed apex.

Variegated horsetail
Equisetum variegatum

or

A sparsely-branched or unbranched plant which does not match all of the previous descriptions (although it may correspond to one or more). Look around you for similar shoots which do have branches, and check them against the marsh horsetail, which usually keys out further on (see D10, page 35).

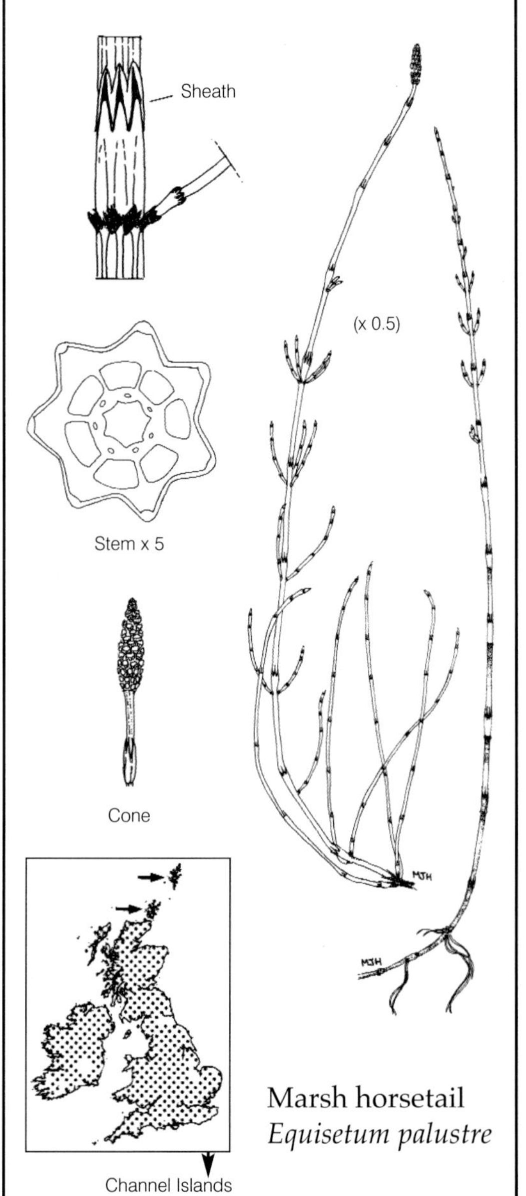

Marsh horsetail
Equisetum palustre

D7 **↑D3** Side branches are more-or-less rigid, borne horizontally or ascending.

or Side branches are slender with a tendency to arch outwards and downwards.

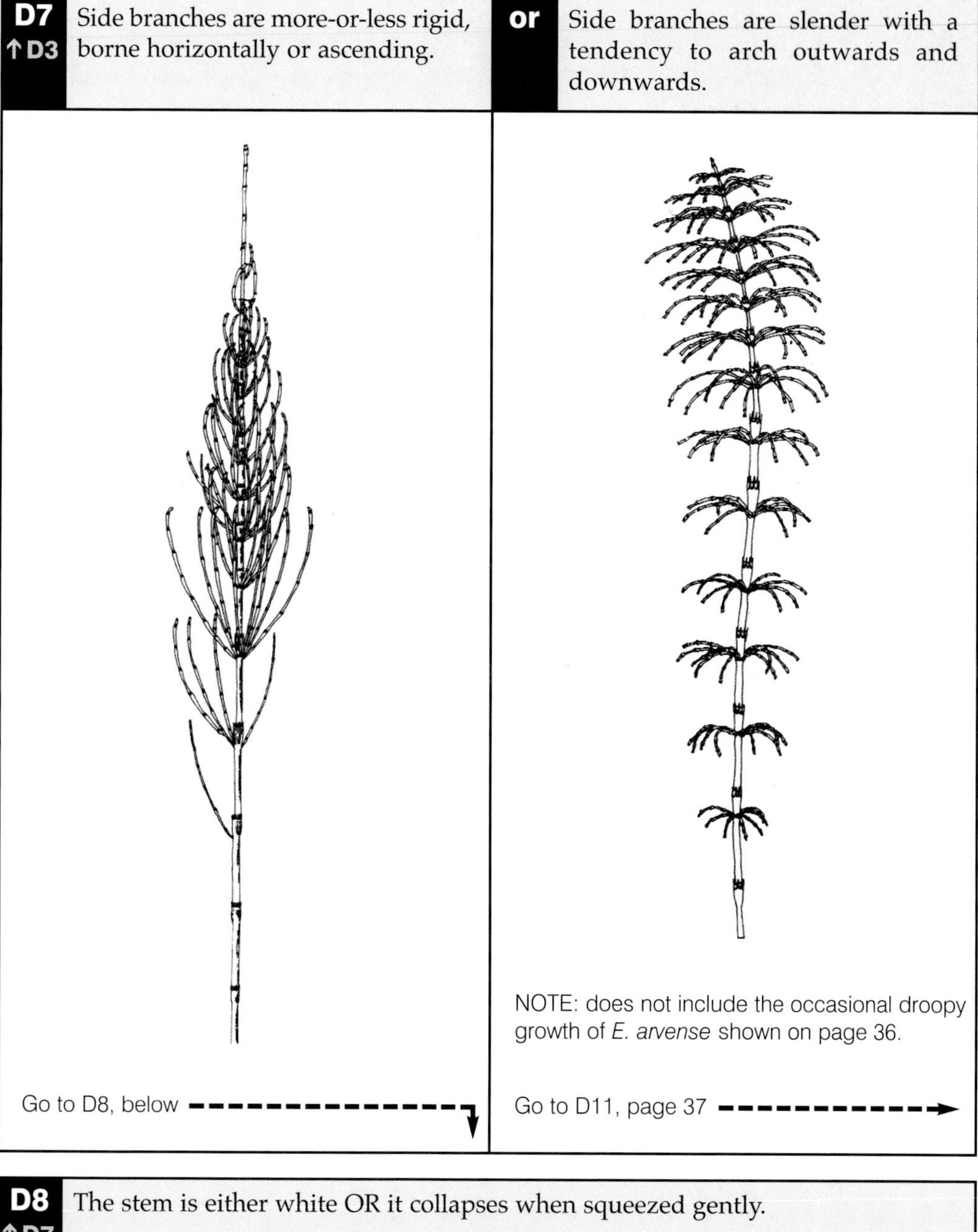

NOTE: does not include the occasional droopy growth of *E. arvense* shown on page 36.

Go to D8, below

Go to D11, page 37

D8 **↑D7** The stem is either white OR it collapses when squeezed gently.

Go to D9, opposite

or The stem is neither white nor collapses when squeezed gently.

Go to D10, page 35

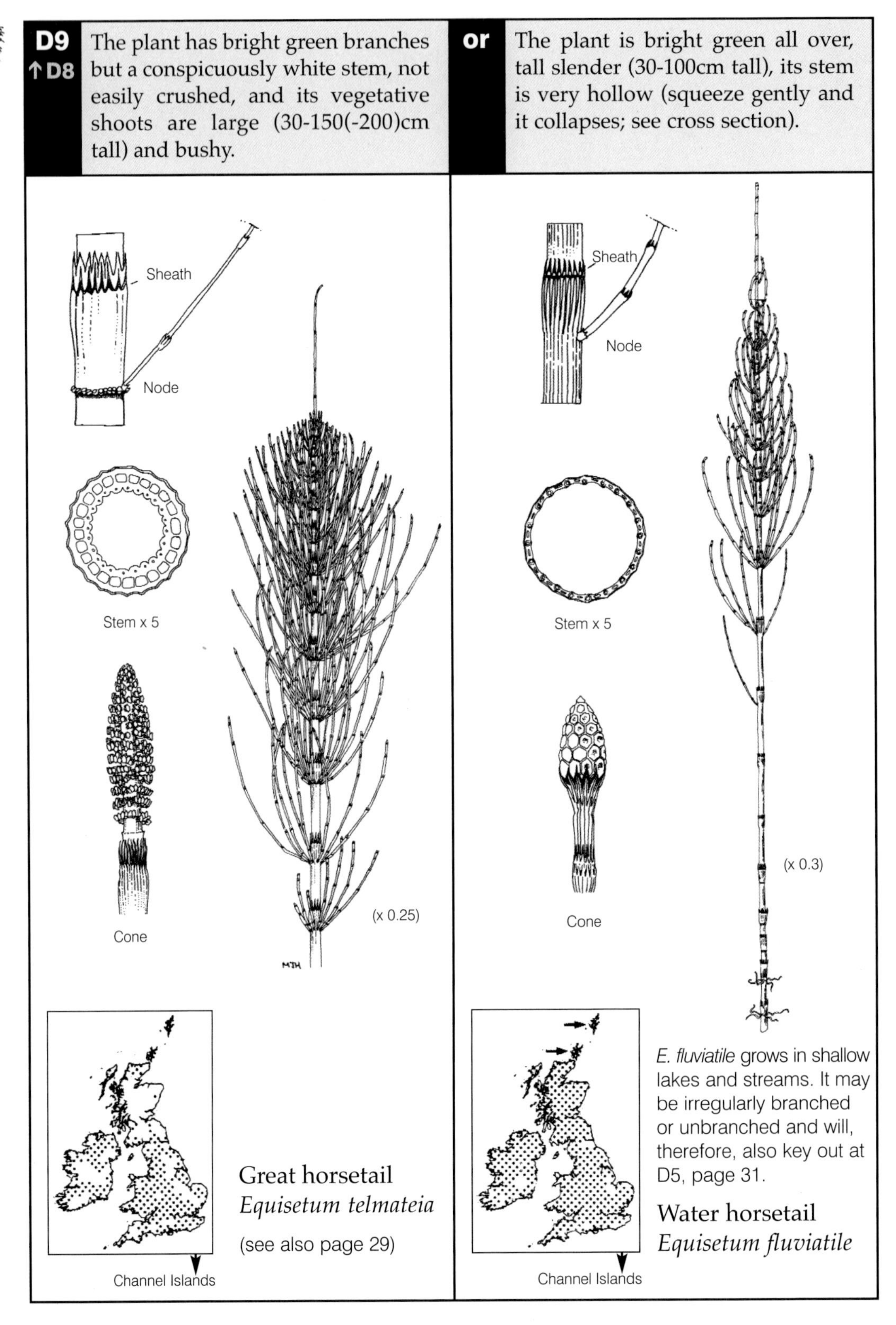
D9
↑D8
The plant has bright green branches but a conspicuously white stem, not easily crushed, and its vegetative shoots are large (30-150(-200)cm tall) and bushy.
or
The plant is bright green all over, tall slender (30-100cm tall), its stem is very hollow (squeeze gently and it collapses; see cross section).
Sheath
Node
Stem x 5
Cone
(x 0.25)
Channel Islands
Great horsetail
Equisetum telmateia
(see also page 29)
Sheath
Node
Stem x 5
Cone
(x 0.3)
E. fluviatile grows in shallow lakes and streams. It may be irregularly branched or unbranched and will, therefore, also key out at D5, page 31.
Water horsetail
Equisetum fluviatile
Channel Islands

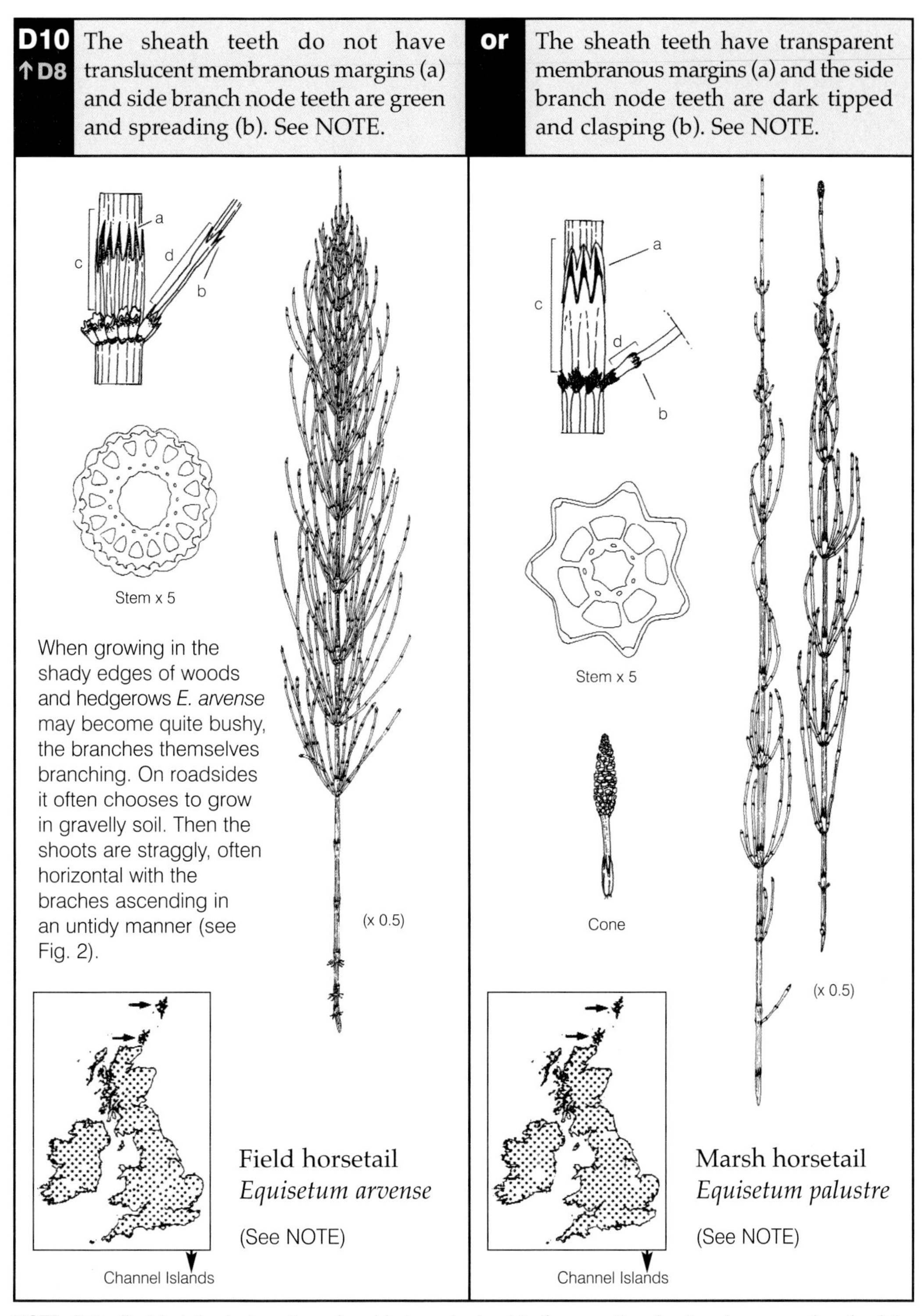

D10 **↑D8** The sheath teeth do not have translucent membranous margins (a) and side branch node teeth are green and spreading (b). See NOTE.

or The sheath teeth have transparent membranous margins (a) and the side branch node teeth are dark tipped and clasping (b). See NOTE.

When growing in the shady edges of woods and hedgerows *E. arvense* may become quite bushy, the branches themselves branching. On roadsides it often chooses to grow in gravelly soil. Then the shoots are straggly, often horizontal with the braches ascending in an untidy manner (see Fig. 2).

Field horsetail
Equisetum arvense

(See NOTE)

Marsh horsetail
Equisetum palustre

(See NOTE)

NOTE: Pull off all but the last section of a side branch about halfway up the shoot and compare length of the remaining section (d) with the height of the leaf sheath on the main stem (c). In *E. arvense* 'd' is equal to or longer than 'c', while in *E. palustre* 'd' is shorter than 'c'.

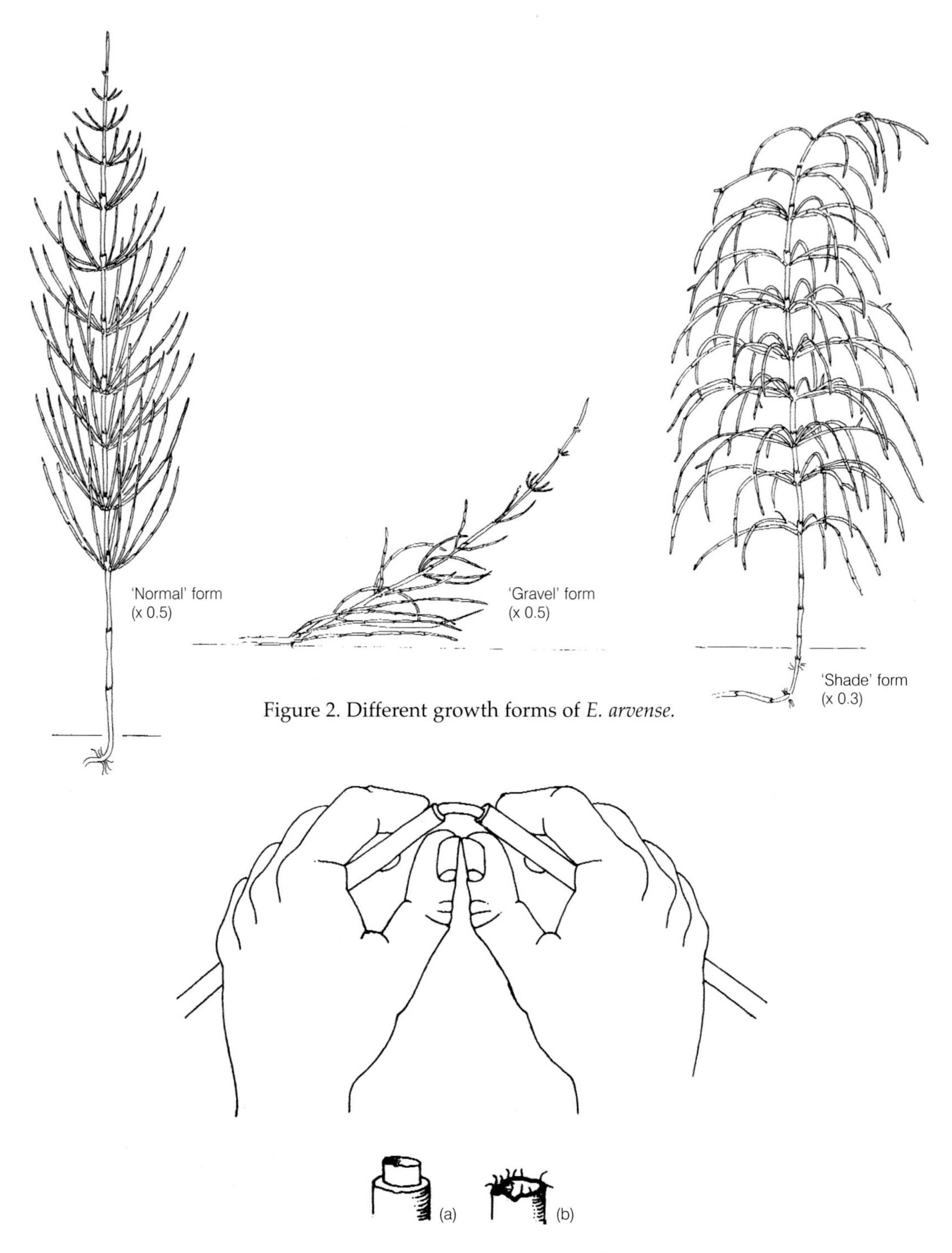

Figure 2. Different growth forms of *E. arvense.*

Figure 3. Separating *E. arvense* and *E.* x *littorale*. The following method can help confirm identification: break the stem across your thumbs between nodes, twisting and pulling as you do so. The outer cylinder of *E. arvense* will part revealing a tough, white inner cylinder which eventually gives way within the node (a). *E.* x *littorale* will simply rip apart and thread-like vascular strands will project from the ragged-edged break (b). After P.G. Barnes (personal communication).

D11
↑D7

Branches are themselves branched; the stem sheaths are inflated and their teeth fused into 4–5 papery lobes which fit very loosely around the stem.

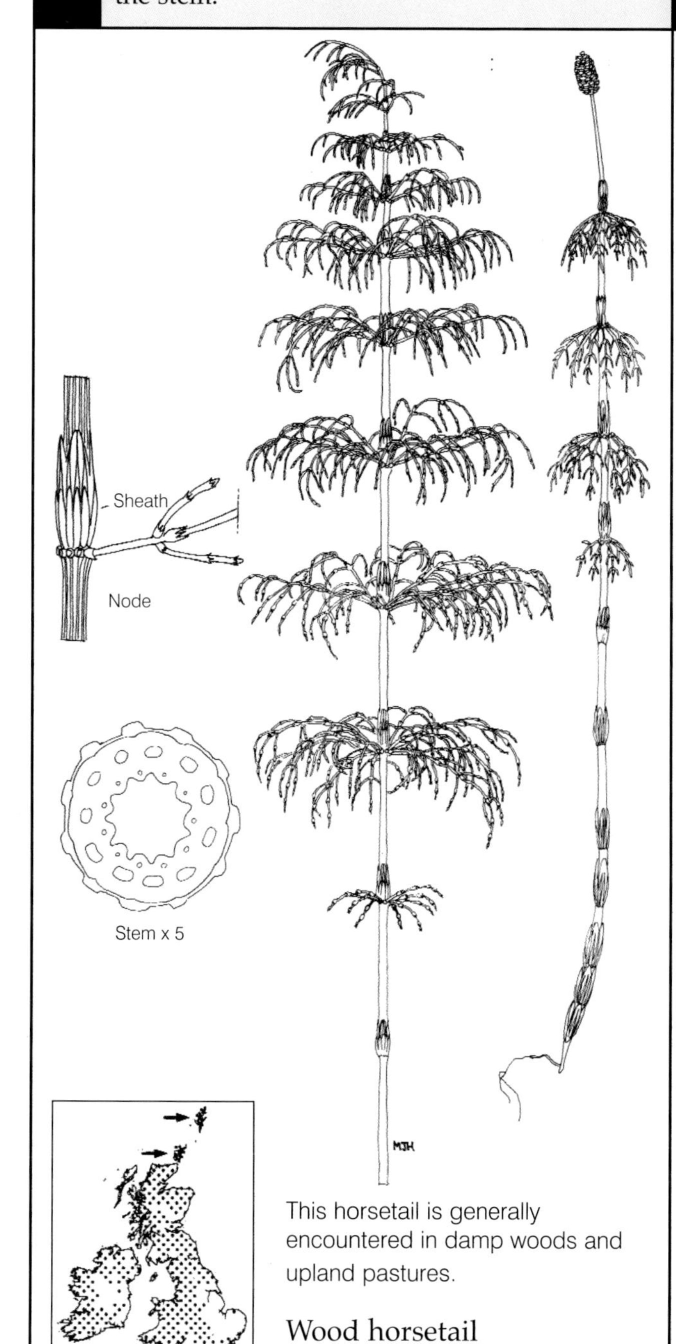

This horsetail is generally encountered in damp woods and upland pastures.

Wood horsetail
Equisetum sylvaticum

or

Branches are unbranched; the sheath teeth are numerous and unfused.

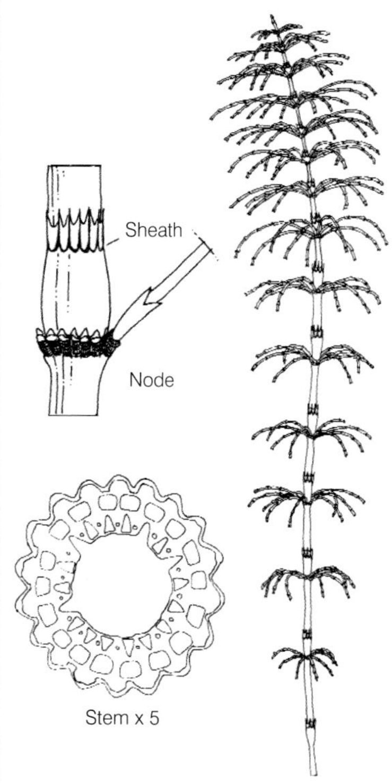

E. pratense is a rare plant of northern England and Scotland where it is to be found on shady river and stream banks. In the shade, the branches of *E. arvense* may be long and drooping, even a little sub-branched. Attention to sheath detail will ensure the correct identification.

Shade Horsetail
Equisetum pratense

KEYS TO BRITISH FERNS

FIRST

Please take a little time to familiarise yourself with these few technical terms.

Frond: Fern leaf.

Indusia (singular *indusium*): Protective membranes of sori which protect the sporangia.

Pinnae (singular *pinna*): First level segment of a fern frond (*see* STEP 1 *overleaf*).

Pinnule: Second level segment of a fern frond (*see* STEP 1 *overleaf*).

Pinnulet: Third level segment of a fern frond (*see* STEP 1 *overleaf*).

Rachis: Midrib of frond, excluding the stipe.

Rhizome: Rooting stem upon which fern fronds arise.

Sori (singular *sorus*): The 'dots' on the back of a frond, aggregations of sporangia, usually protected by indusia.

Sporangia (singular *sporangium*): Spore capsules.

Stipe: Stalk, or the non-leafy part of a frond.

THEN

Follow steps 1 to 3 overleaf to obtain a 2-digit frond architecture code which you use to select the appropriate key. In the key, consider the pairs of questions posed, selecting the answer that matches your unknown fern. At each stage you will be instructed where to continue the keying process until you reach the name of your unknown fern.

The illustrations are there to guide you when visual clues are necessary. Do not be tempted to make quick picture matches because it often leads to the wrong identification. If you go wrong, back-track and try again.

Step 1

Determine the degree to which your fern frond is divided and note the number given: 0, 1, 2 or 3. Choose a mature plant with sori. Make your count where the frond is broadest. Pinnae, pinnules or pinnulets are distinct when they are separated down to the midrib.

NB: ***the main axis counts as*** **0**

If the frond is not divided – COUNT 0

If the frond is divided once into distinct pinnae – COUNT 1

If the frond is divided twice into distinct pinnules – COUNT 2

If the frond is divided thrice into distinct pinnulets – COUNT 3

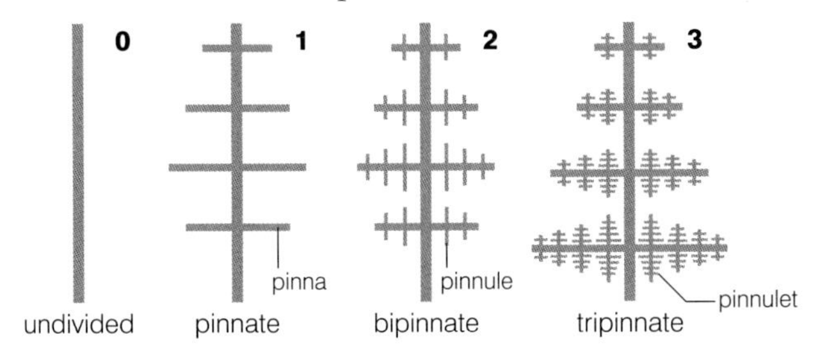

Step 2

Determine fern frond shape by selecting its outline and note the letter given: A, B, C, D or E beside the number for frond division.

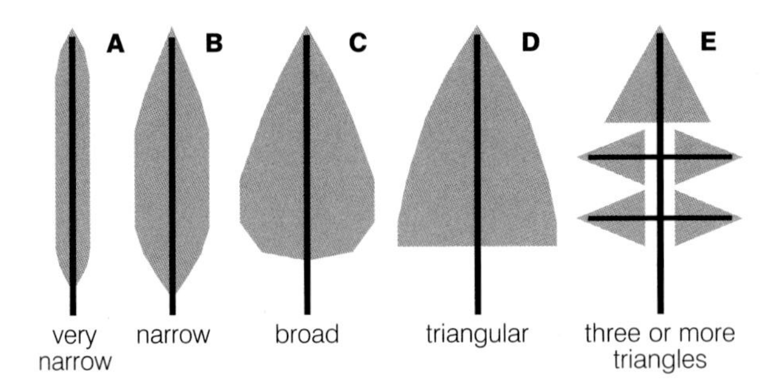

You now have a two digit code for frond architecture e.g. 0A, 2C or 3E. This is given in square brackets in the keys (e.g. [OA]).

Step 3

Look for your 2-digit code in the table below and select the appropriate identification key.

Code	Frond type	Instruction
0A, 0B or 0C	Undivided	Go to **Key E**, page 41
1A, 1B, 1C or 1D	Pinnate	Go to **Key F**, page 44
2A, 2B, 2C, 2D, or 3B	Bipinnate	Go to **Key G**, page 54
3C or 3D	Tripinnate	Go to **Key H**, page 78
3E	Tripinnate-Multipart	Go to **Key I**, page 83

KEY E: FERNS WITH UNDIVIDED FRONDS

E1 The strap-like fronds uncurl as they develop and the linear sori are in two rows, one on either side of the rachis, set obliquely on the underside of the frond. [0A].

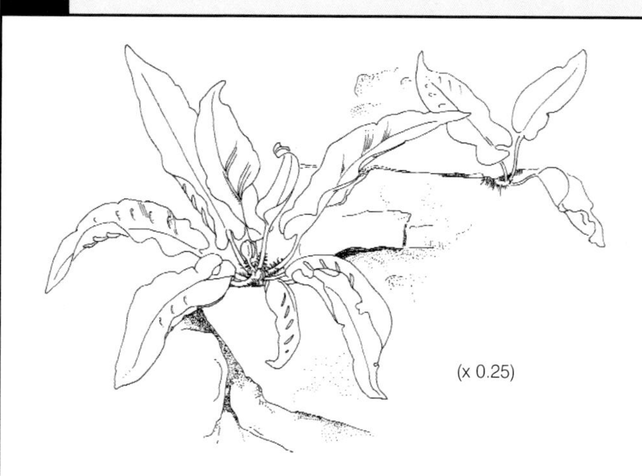

(x 0.25)

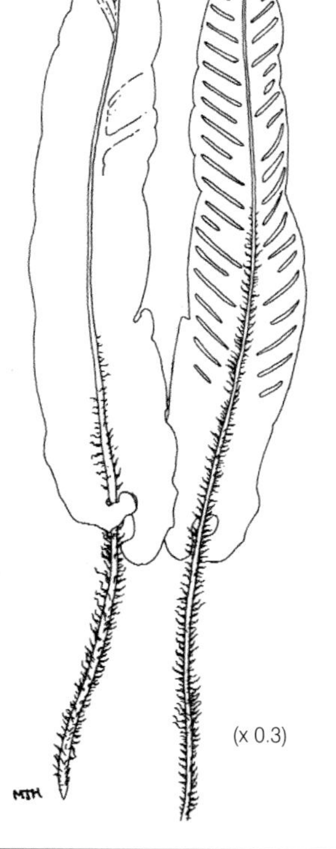

(x 0.3)

Channel Islands

Whilst occuring in neutral or slightly acid habitats, this fern grows best in calcareous woodland and lime-rich rocks and walls (even wells, tombs and drains).

Hart's tongue fern
Asplenium scolopendrium

or The fronds do not uncurl like other ferns and the leaf blade is divided into two: a fertile spike in front of the oval, fleshy blade; growing in meadow or maritime turf (see NOTE at E2).

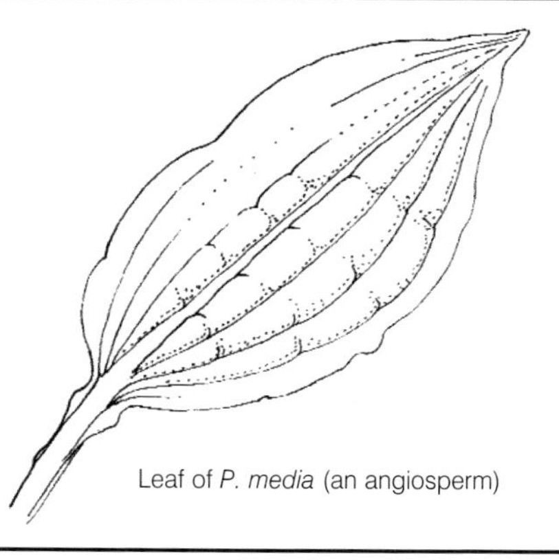

Leaf of *P. media* (an angiosperm)

This lead will take you to the three adder's tongues. Even the largest of the adder's tongues is not easy to find, requiring a careful search, and the leaves of the hoary plantain, *Plantago media*, can cause confusion (see left). However, plantain has distinctively ribbed leaves, whilst our ferns have a faint network of veins, and the leaves are fleshy. To compound the problem the common adder's tongue is frequently found with no fertile spike.

Go to E2, overleaf ------------→

E2 **↑E1** The leaf blade is single (very rarely paired) and usually taller than 10cm. [0B/C].

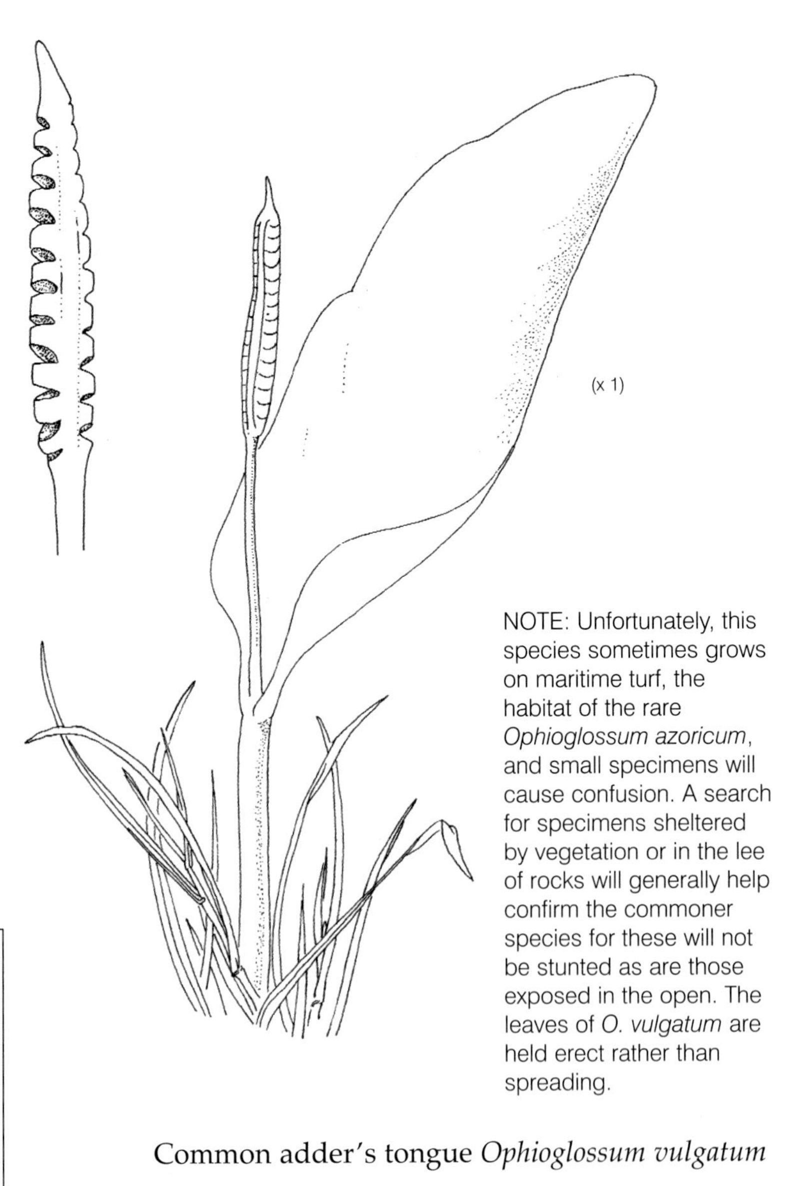

NOTE: Unfortunately, this species sometimes grows on maritime turf, the habitat of the rare *Ophioglossum azoricum*, and small specimens will cause confusion. A search for specimens sheltered by vegetation or in the lee of rocks will generally help confirm the commoner species for these will not be stunted as are those exposed in the open. The leaves of *O. vulgatum* are held erect rather than spreading.

Common adder's tongue *Ophioglossum vulgatum*

or The leaf blade is very small, 3-7cm (single or paired).

Go to E3, opposite →

E3
↑E2

The single leaf is broad (3-5cm x 3-4cm), leaves tending to group in twos and threes. Grows in short turf by the sea. [0B/C].

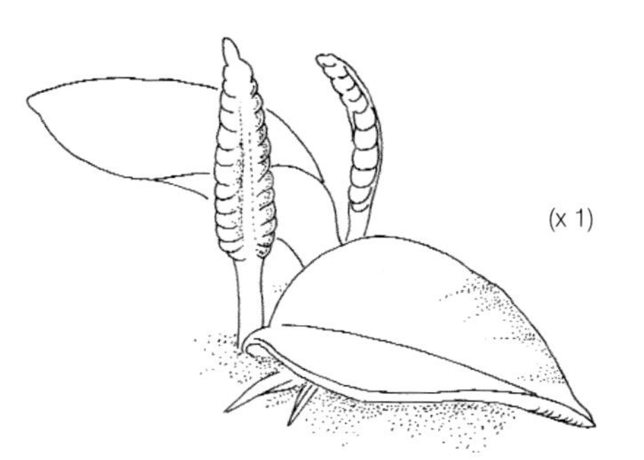

This species is rare and your specimen must be checked carefully, for it may be a stunted *Ophioglossum vulgatum* from which it may be distingushed (not without some difficulty) by its narrower leaf blade with a more tapering base and a more spreading habit (not as strong as in *O. lusitanicum* below).

Smaller adder's tongue *Ophioglossum azoricum*

or

The single, sometimes paired leaves are narow (3-7 x 1-2cm) and very fleshy. Only in Guernsey (where all three adder's tongues grow) and the Isles of Scilly. [0B/C].

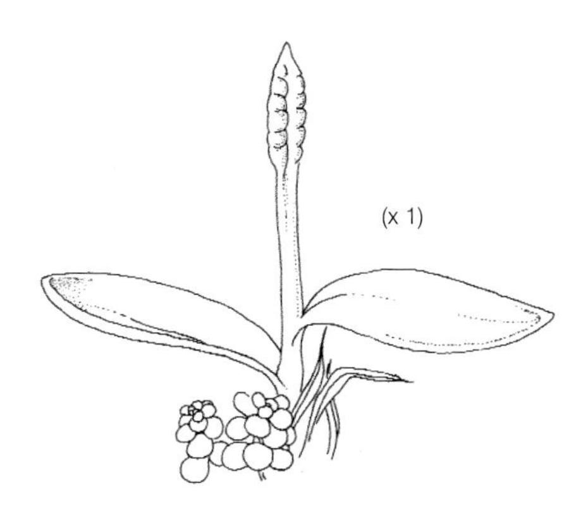

The very rare *O. lusitanicum* differs from the other two by having leaves which spread across the soil surface rather than being held erect on their stems. It is to be found above ground from November, dying away in April.

Least adders's tongue *Ophioglossum lusitanicum*

KEY F: FERNS WITH ONCE DIVIDED, PINNATE FRONDS

F1 The leaf blade is irregularly forked; a rare fern of nutrient-poor mountain rocks and lowland walls where its slender, grey-green leaves form dense tufts. [1A/B].

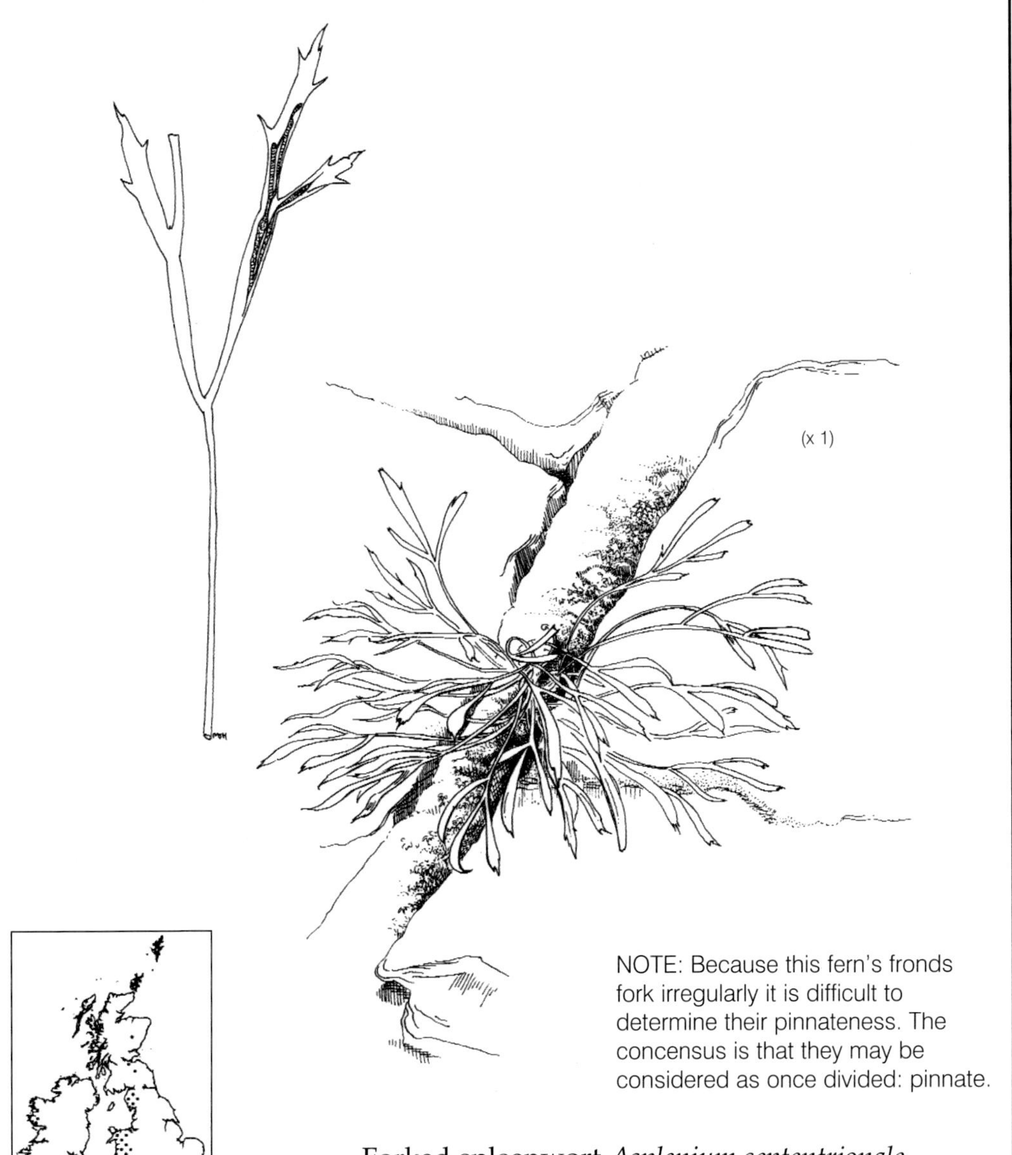

NOTE: Because this fern's fronds fork irregularly it is difficult to determine their pinnateness. The concensus is that they may be considered as once divided: pinnate.

Forked spleenwort *Asplenium septentrionale*

or The leaf blade is divided regularly.

Go to F2, opposite ------→

F2
↑F1

The fleshy 5-35cm high leaves with fan-shaped pinnae are found emerging singly from upland turf (less frequently lowland) and each has a fertile spike emerging from the blade base. [1A].

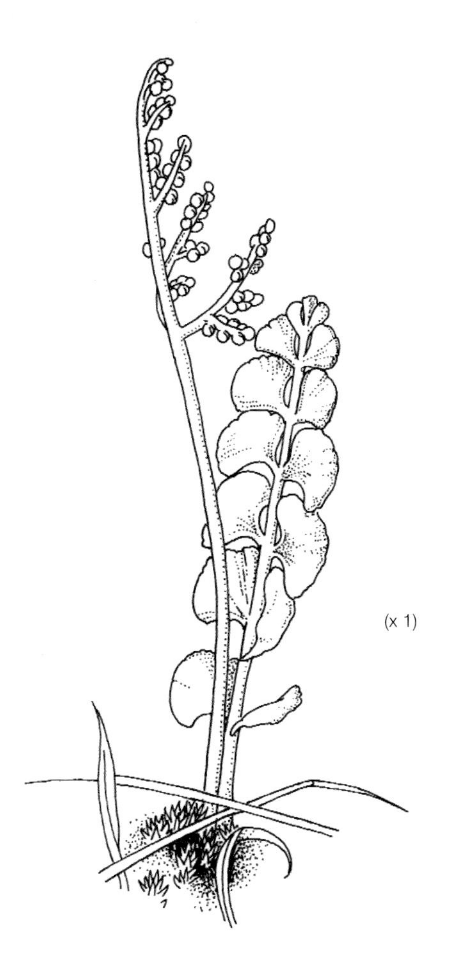

(x 1)

The moonwort has found its way into folklore. It may be used as the key to open any lock and, if you are rash enough to gallop your horse over turf where it is growing, beware: the horseshoes will fall off!

Moonwort *Botrychium lunaria*

or

If not as above, i.e. the specimen does not have all the characters described above.

Go to F3, overleaf ➔

F3
↑F2

The pinnae are hard, toothed and prickly; on lime-rich mountains, usually at altitudes greater than 500m (a rare plant). [1A].

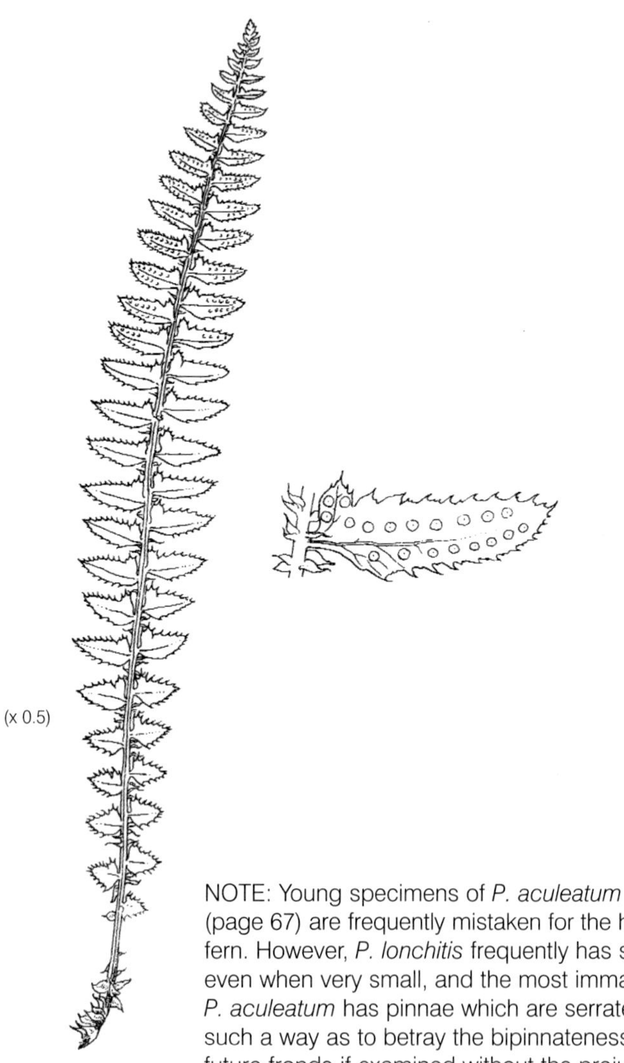

NOTE: Young specimens of *P. aculeatum* (page 67) are frequently mistaken for the holly fern. However, *P. lonchitis* frequently has sori, even when very small, and the most immature *P. aculeatum* has pinnae which are serrated in such a way as to betray the bipinnateness of future fronds if examined without the prejudice of one who desperately wishes to find the rarer species.

Holly fern *Polystichum lonchitis*

or

The pinnae are not distinctly prickly.

Go to F4, opposite ——————→

F4
↑ F3

The frond undersurface has a dense covering of rust-brown scales (silvery when the fronds are new) around and over the sori. [1A].

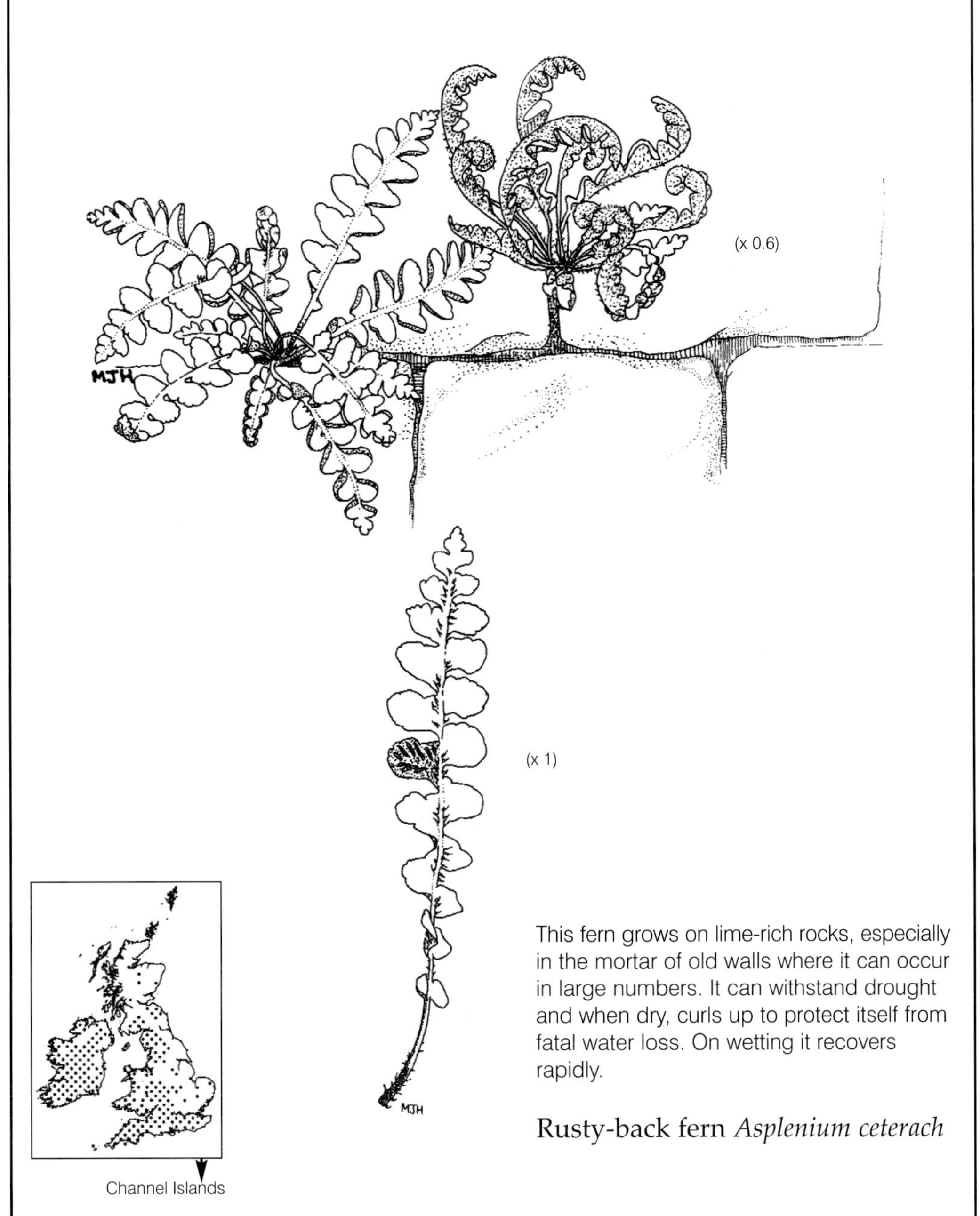

This fern grows on lime-rich rocks, especially in the mortar of old walls where it can occur in large numbers. It can withstand drought and when dry, curls up to protect itself from fatal water loss. On wetting it recovers rapidly.

Rusty-back fern *Asplenium ceterach*

or

The frond undersurface is not densely scaly.

Go to F5, overleaf ⟶

F5
↑F4

The plants form rosettes on peaty soils, and the fronds are long and narrow (15-30(-50) x 2-5cm) lanceolate, firm and rigid to touch, but not prickly. In mature plants the sterile and spore bearing (fertile) fronds are different. [1A].

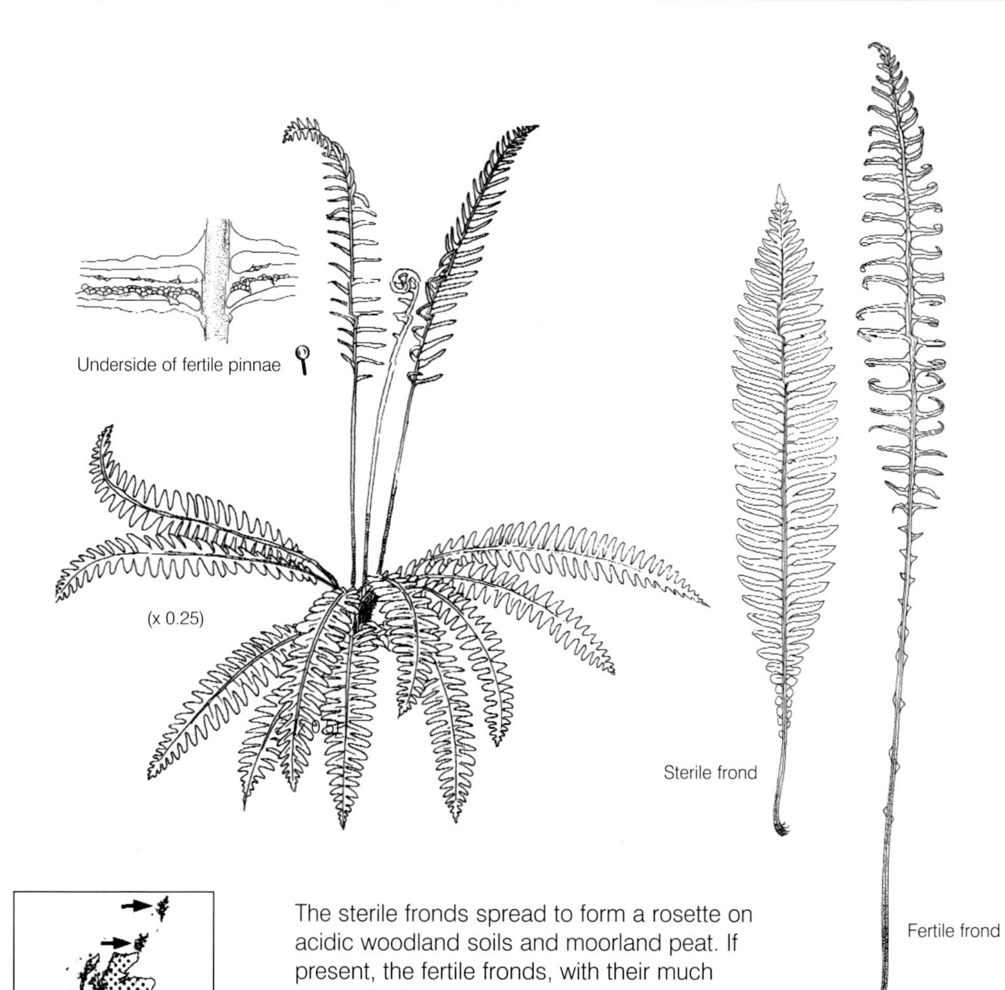

The sterile fronds spread to form a rosette on acidic woodland soils and moorland peat. If present, the fertile fronds, with their much narrower pinnae, thrust dramatically up through the centre of the rosette; in these plants, the fronds will be up to three times the size of those illustrated.

Hard fern *Blechnum spicant*

or

The plant is not a rosette former and it grows on walls, trees or among rocks, but never on peaty soils (all fronds similar).

Go to F6, opposite →

F6
↑F5

The fronds arise at intervals from a creeping rhizome which may be seen (and can be felt) running along the surface.

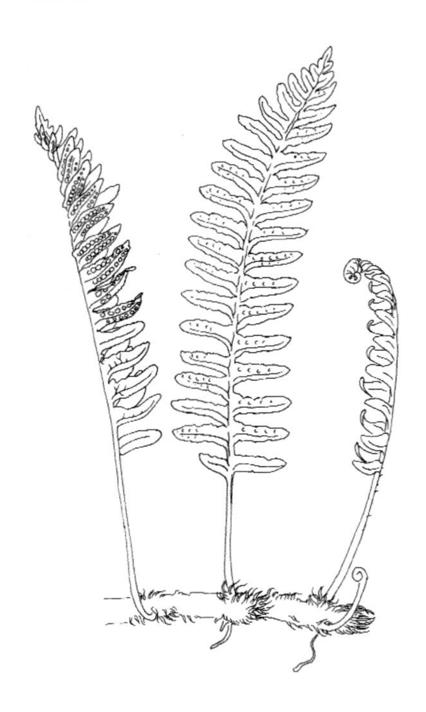

Go to F7 →

or

The fronds are clustered to form a tuft.

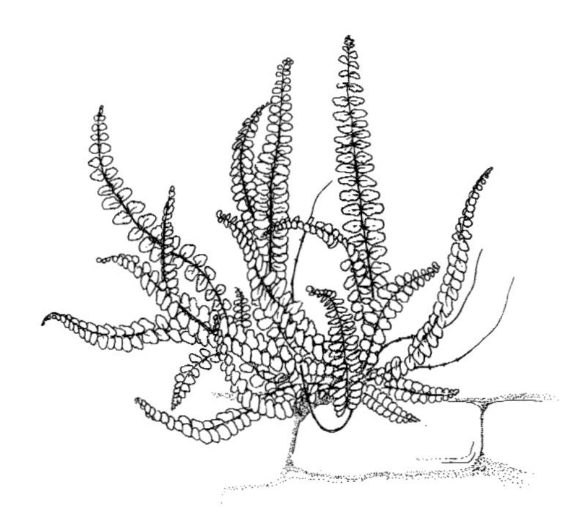

Go to F8, page 52 →

F7
↑F6

The three British polypoides are closely related and rather alike which makes field identification difficult but by no means impossible. A microscope is needed for 100% confidence. They all have a scaly rhizome which creeps among rocks, on walls and in hedge banks. They may also grow on trees in sheltered localities.

Rather than continue the dichotomous key here it has been thought more practical to provide a table to the features by which each species is uniquely characterised.

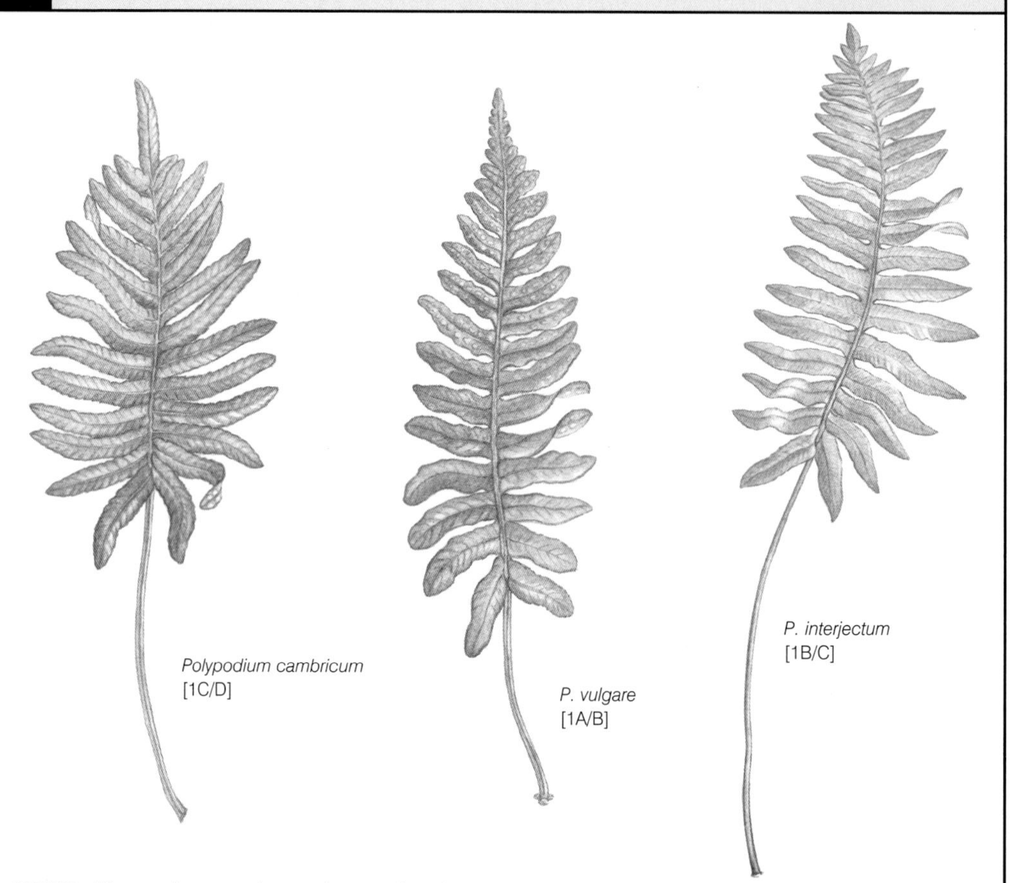

NOTE: Not only are there three closely-related and similar species of *Polypodium* in Britain, but also they hybridise, providing a confusing matrix of established species and intermediates. If one encounters an outsize polypodium (hybrid vigour) which has a combination of the features of two parents examine the back of a mature frond with a hand lens to establish the condition of the sporangia and their spores. Hybrids are unable to produce healthy spores which end up shrivelled and useless. The sori are few, small and purplish in colour, a stark contrast with the plump green, becoming golden sori of the species polypoides. The hybrids *P. vulgare* x *P. cambricum* (*P.* x *font-queri*) and *P. interjectum* x *P. cambricum* (*P.* x *shivasiae*) are not frequently encountered, partly because of the limited distribution of *P. cambricum*, but they may occasionally be found where the parents co-habit. The third hybrid, *P. vulgare* x *P. interjectum* (*P.* x *mantoniae*) is very widespread and, the more one is aware of it, the commoner it seems to be. It is an extremely robust plant and though, like the other two hybrids it produces non-viable spores, it is a long-lived, rampantly-spreading plant which may even out-compete its own parents.

Continue overleaf ------------------------------------→

F7 Continued.

	Polypodium cambricum Southern polypody	*Polypodium vulgare* Common polypody	*Polypodium interjectum* Western polypody
Distribution	Mostly south and west Britain	Thoughout	Mostly western Britain
Habitat	Limestone	Acid rocks and soils	Weakly acid or basic rocks and soils
Sporangium	When sporangium young, annulus brown, paraphyses present	When sporangium young, annulus golden brown, paraphyses absent	When sporangium young, annulus yellow-green, indistinct, paraphyses absent
Pinnae	Apex acute. Margins ± serrated	Apex blunt. Margins ± entire	Apex acute. Margins ± serrated
Sori	Oval. Green, then pale yellow, later brown	± circular. Green, soon golden, later brown	Oval. Green, then pale yellow, later brown
Lowest pair pinnae	Strongly inflexed	Flat or weakly inflexed	Strongly inflexed
Leaf outline	Broadly ovate to triangular (see opposite)	Narrow ovate. Often ± parallel-sided (see opposite)	Ovate (see opposite)

F8
↑F6

Plant with glossy, fleshy fronds, growing in fissures and cavities in cliffs, walls, or rocks by the sea (within the sea spray zone). [1A].

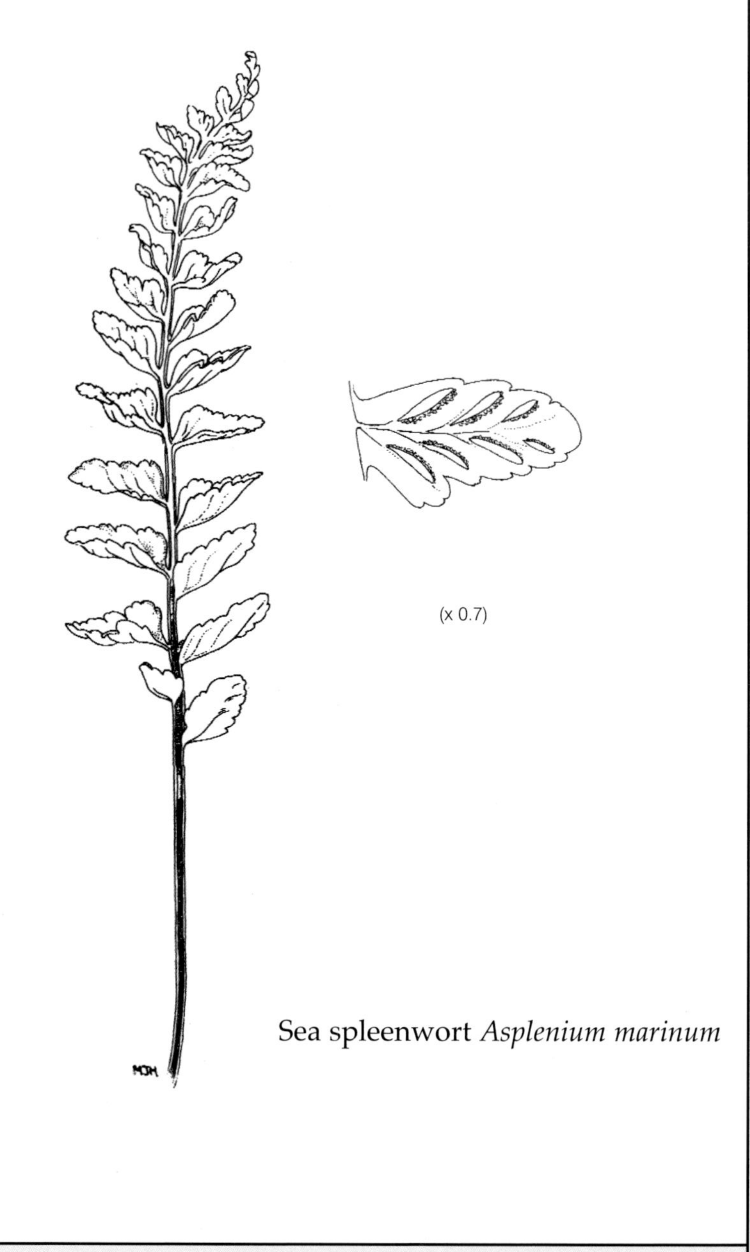

Sea spleenwort *Asplenium marinum*

or

Plant neither glossy nor fleshy-leaved, and not growing within the sea spray zone.

Go to F9, opposite ⟶

F9
↑F8

The yellow-green to dark green (not lime-green) pinnae are borne on a wiry, dark brown rachis. [1A].

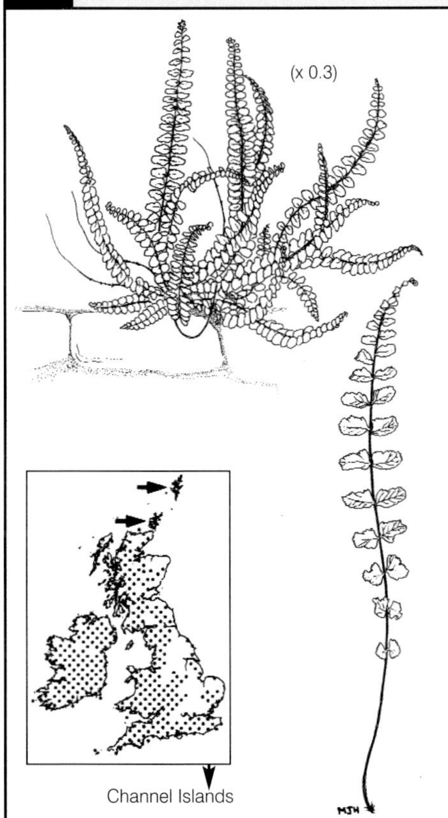

The maidenhair spleenwort forms dense tufts on rocks and walls and often has dead stalks amongst its fronds.

NOTE: There are three British subspecies of this fern. The commonest, *Asplenium trichomanes* subsp, *quadrivalens*, grows on lime-rich rocks and in the mortar in walls. Its pinnae are oblong and inserted at an angle to the flat of the frond. They remain on the rachis until the whole frond is shed in winter. The second, *Asplenium trichomanes* subsp. *trichomanes*, is less common and prefers a more-or-less lime-free habitat. It is an altogether smaller and more slender plant with rounded pinnae which are held in the plane of the frond, and, at the end of the season, fall from their persistent stalks, leaving them to remain untidily among the new fronds. The third, which has been known for some time in south-central Europe, *Asplenium trichomanes* subsp. *pachyrachis*, has recently been found in south-east Wales, western England and Yorkshire. It grows in cracks in shady limestone crags and walls where its fronds press close to the rock. The crowded pinnae are incised with a triangular outline.

Maidenhair spleenwort
Asplenium trichomanes

or

The lime-green pinnae are borne on a green rachis. [1A].

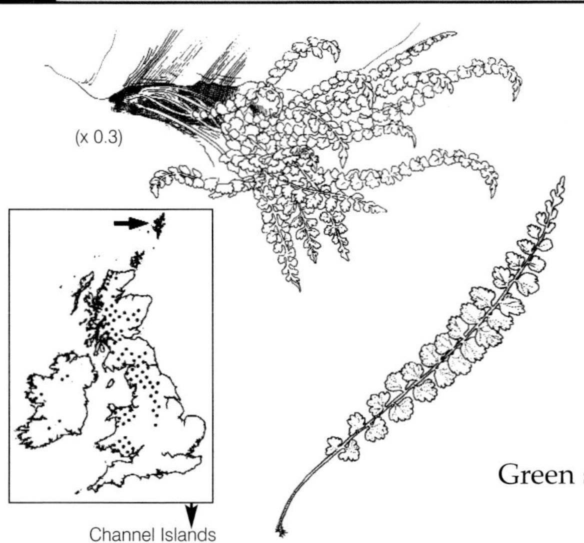

Asplenium viride is a tufted fern of lime-rich upland rocks and wet alpine flushes. Its pinnae are rounded, fan-shaped, the rachis persistent.

NOTE: The fronds of *A. viride* are soft, often hanging in cascades under shady mountain rocks wheras those of *A. trichomanes* are wiry, giving that fern an altogether more 'bristling' appearance.

Green spleenwort *Asplenium viride*

KEY G: FERNS WITH TWICE DIVIDED, BIPINNATE FRONDS

G1 The frond is very thin, delicate and virtually transparent (for it is only one cell thick between the veins). The plant is one of the filmy ferns.

Go to G2 →

or The frond is opaque and obviously more than one cell thick.

Go to G4, page 57 →

G2
↑G1

The broadly-triangular, finely-divided frond is 5-15(-30)cm long and the sporangia are borne upon a bristle which emerges from a cup-like structure on the leaf margin. [2/3D].

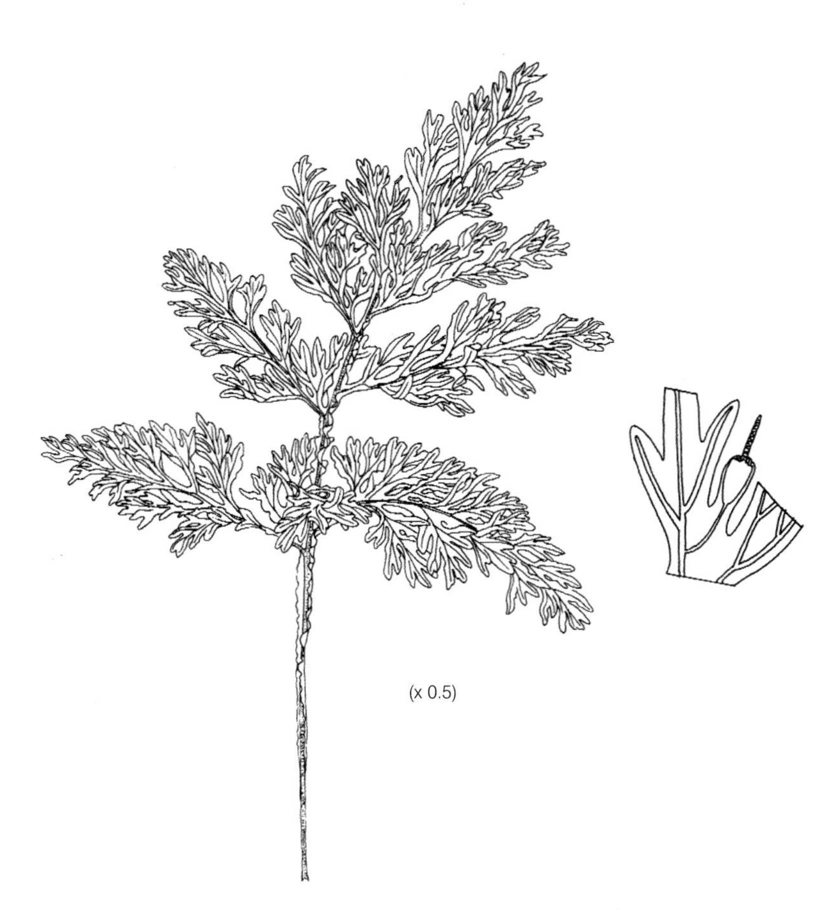

(x 0.5)

This beautiful fern is so rare, as a result of appalling over collection by Victorian fanatics, that the sporophyte is now found only in a handful of sites in Britain. *Trichomanes speciosum* is now thoroughly protected by law and these precious few sites kept secret.

Killarney bristle fern *Trichomanes speciosum*

or

The fronds are ovate or oblong in outline, sometimes being less than 5cm long, and the sporangia are borne between paired indusia.

Go to G3, overleaf →

G3
↑ G2

The ovate fronds are only 2-5cm long, gently narrowing to the tip and the sporangia are enclosed between paired circular indusia, the edges of which are toothed. [2B/C].

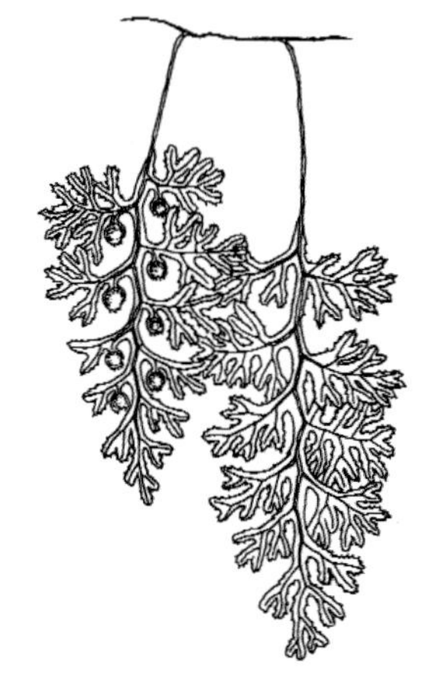

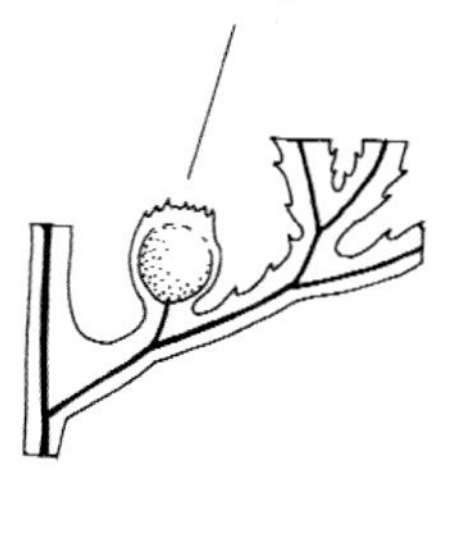

Tunbridge filmy fern *Hymenophyllum tunbrigense*
(Plate 8)

or

The oblong fronds are only 2-10cm long with a blunt or almost spreading tip, and the sporangia are enclosed between paired oval indusia, the edges of which are not toothed. [2B/C].

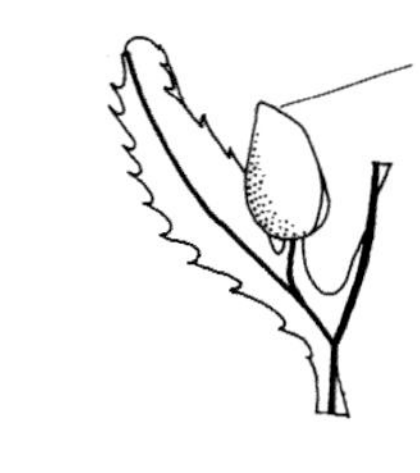

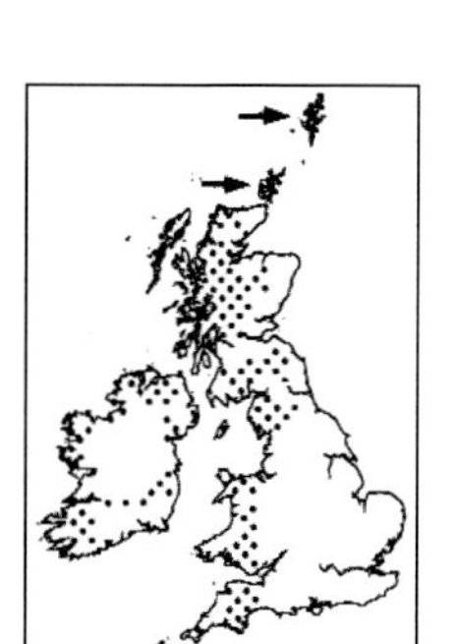

NOTE: Whereas the lower pinnae of *H. tunbrigense* fan out more-or-less equally to both sides of the main vein, those of *H. wilsonii* tend to be unequal, spreading mostly in the direction of the leaf tip.

Wilson's filmy fern *Hymenophyllum wilsonii*
(Plate 8)

NOTE: The two species of *Hymenophyllum* are small and frequently grow with mosses from which they may be difficult to tell apart (see Plate 8). Only close examination will reveal that these filmy ferns have fully veined leaves and their characteristic sori.

G4
↑G1

The frond is divided into spreading fan-shaped segments.

Three examples out of three

Go to G5. page 58 →

or

The frond is divided into lanceolate, ovate or oblong pinnae.

Three examples out of twenty-three

Go to G7, page 60 →

G5
↑G4

Medium sized plant, the fronds up to 30cm arising from (often hanging down) a creeping rhizome. The leaf stalks are dark brown and wiry. [2C/D].

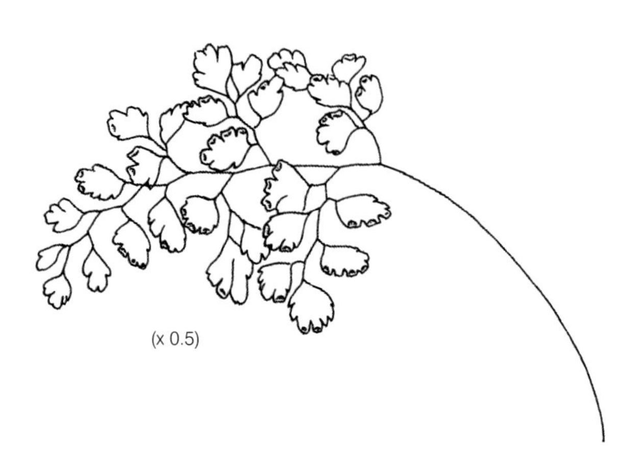

The sori are at the pinna margins where the pale, membranous indusium looks as if it is the edge of the pinna folded under. This species is more common on the continent than in Britain. Here it is a rather rare fern of coastal cliffs where it grows sheltered from direct sea spray. Many species of maidenhair fern are popular house plants.

Maidenhair fern
Adiantum capillus-veneris

or

Small plant, the fronds less than 10cm long arising from an upright rhizome; the leaf stalks not wiry.

Go to G6, opposite →

G6
↑G5

Diminutive fern (usually less than 10cm) with very little rhizome, the stipes yellow-green and linear sori, which lack indusia, radiating along the pinna veins. Channel Islands only. [2B/C].

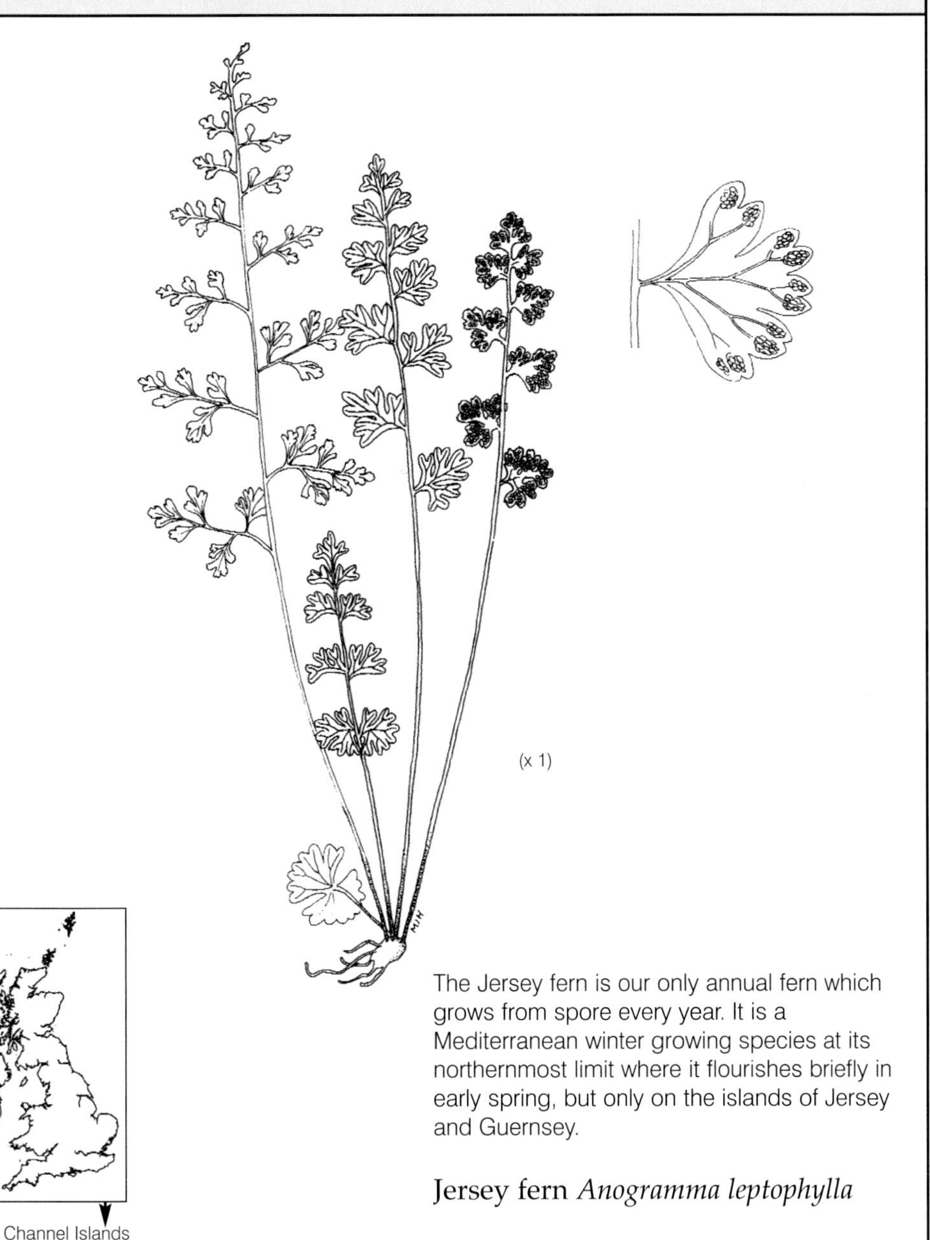

The Jersey fern is our only annual fern which grows from spore every year. It is a Mediterranean winter growing species at its northernmost limit where it flourishes briefly in early spring, but only on the islands of Jersey and Guernsey.

Jersey fern *Anogramma leptophylla*

or

A small tufted fern (up to 10cm) of inland walls and lime-rich rocks, the frond irregularly bipinnate with diamond-, fan-shaped or rounded pinnules.

Wall rue *Asplenium ruta-muraria* (see G12, page 63)

G7
↑G4

A strikingly large fern, fronds 60-150cm high, emerging from a raised mound created by the erect rhizome, with broad, light green pinnae, bearing its large sporangia (⚲ not necessary) like erect bunches of grapes at the frond apex.

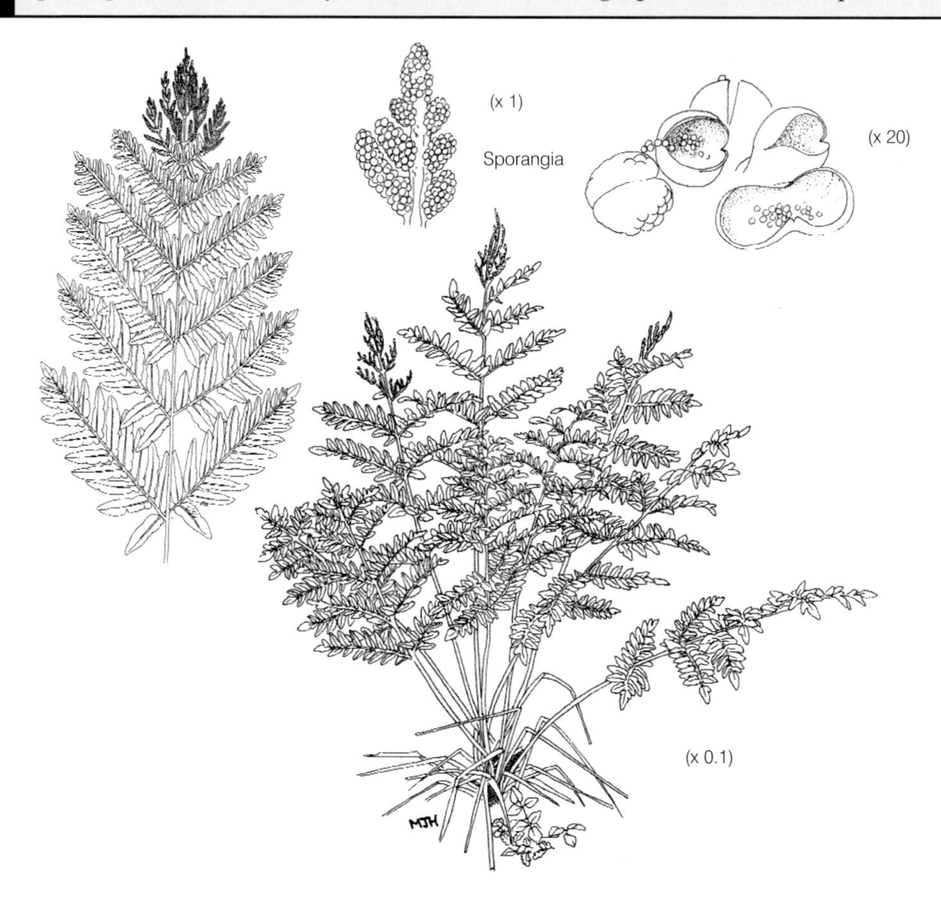

Osmunda is an increasingly rare fern of acidic bogs and fenny woodlands, suffering badly from insensitive collection in the past and habitat destruction today. It does not always attain the maximum stature given above but, when it does, plants several metres in circumference, the fronds of which arch over the pteridologist's head, are to be found at some sites. *Osmunda* also grows on sea cliffs where one may find small plants which establish themselves for a decade or so on wet rock faces until they outgrow this temporary habitat.

Royal fern *Osmunda regalis*

or Without all of the characters described above.

Go to G8, opposite --→

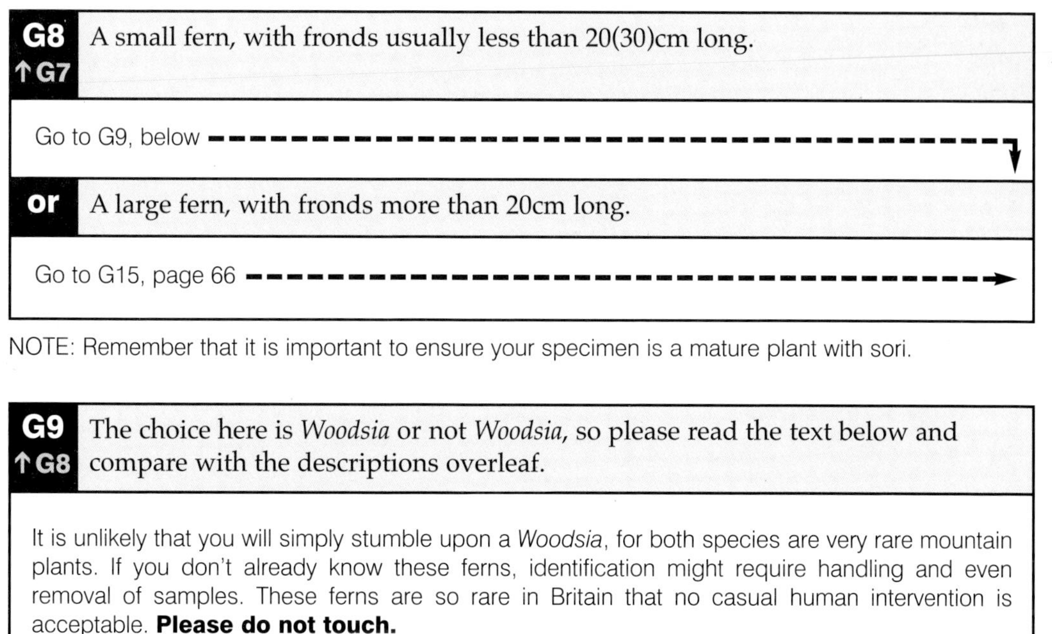

G8 **↑G7** A small fern, with fronds usually less than 20(30)cm long.

Go to G9, below

or A large fern, with fronds more than 20cm long.

Go to G15, page 66

NOTE: Remember that it is important to ensure your specimen is a mature plant with sori.

G9 **↑G8** The choice here is *Woodsia* or not *Woodsia*, so please read the text below and compare with the descriptions overleaf.

It is unlikely that you will simply stumble upon a *Woodsia*, for both species are very rare mountain plants. If you don't already know these ferns, identification might require handling and even removal of samples. These ferns are so rare in Britain that no casual human intervention is acceptable. **Please do not touch.**

Instead, visually check against the descriptions and illustrations opposite and, if you have found *Woodsia*, you should be able to decide which one it is without touching. By all means enjoy it and record it, but only with your eyes, memory and camera.

If *Woodsia* Go to G10, overleaf

If not *Woodsia* Go to G11, page 63

G10 ↑ **G9** The pinnae are oblong – one and a half times to twice as long as broad and the frond surface is clothed with long scales and hairs. [2A].

Oblong woodsia *Woodsia ilvensis* (see NOTE)

or The pinnae are triangular – no more than one and a half as long as broad – and frond undersurface bears sparse scales or hairs. [2A].

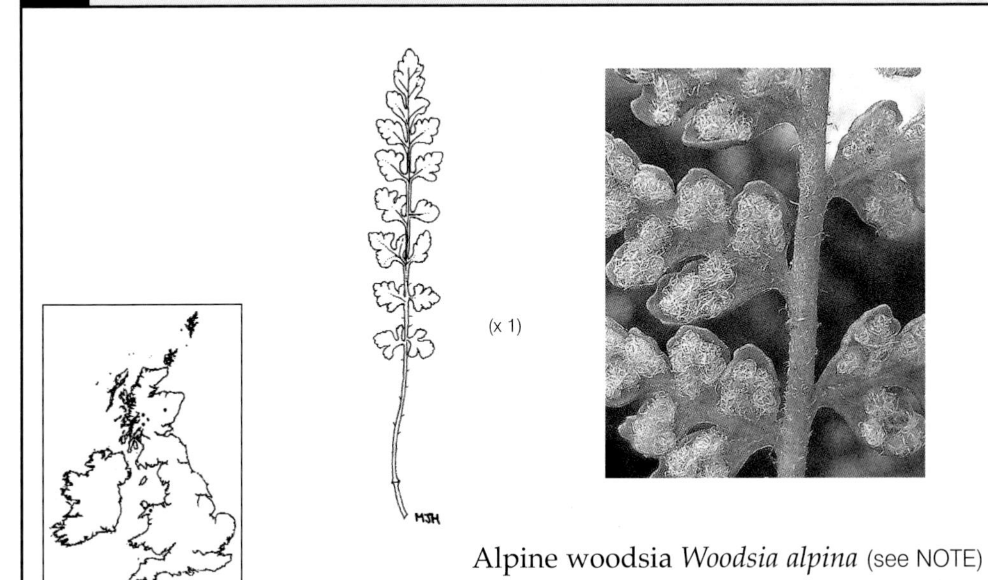

Alpine woodsia *Woodsia alpina* (see NOTE)

NOTE: Either of the woodsias may be confused with young plants of *Cystopteris fragilis* (see G13). Carefully inspect the indusium for in *Woodsia* it has a filamentous margin (appears 'hairy'), whereas in *Cystopteris* it is hood-like or absent because it has shrivelled away.

G11 **↑G9** The sori are linear, the indusium an elongate flap.

Go to G12, below

or The sori are more-or-less circular, the indusium shrivelling and disappearing early (so that most species appear to have no indusium).

Go to G13, overleaf

NOTE: You are unlikely to find yourself faced with a specimen with no sori and no others in the vicinity to allow verification. If, however, you do find yourself in this situation, you must briefly break the rule and compare it against the illustrations of the next five species in the key.

G12 **↑G11** Small tufted plant (up to 10cm) of inland walls and lime-rich rocks, the frond irregularly bipinnate with diamond-shaped, fan-shaped or rounded pinnules. [2B/C].

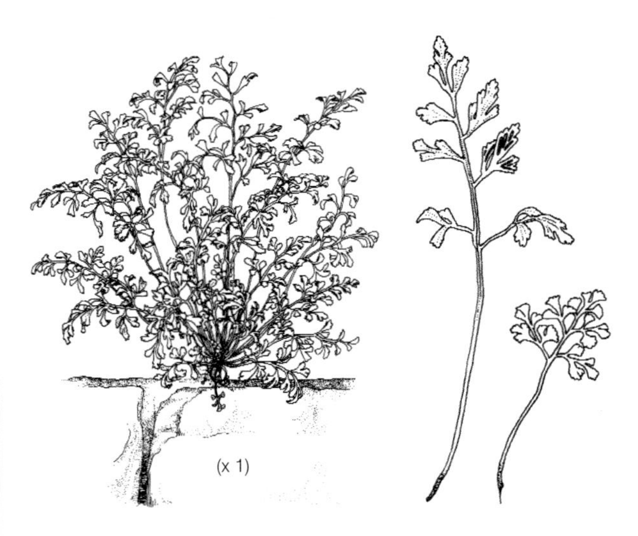

Wall rue *Asplenium ruta-muraria*

or Medium sized plant (10-30cm), the frond regularly bipinnate (possibly tripinnate) and the pinnules are not notably diamond-, fan-shaped or rounded.

Go to G14. page 65

G13
↑G11

Fern forms loose, often cascading tufts on limestone rocks or mortared walls or by lime-rich mountain flushes. [2B/C].

Early in the season, the sori of *C. fragilis* are covered by indusia which resemble hoods or minute bottles but they soon shrivel and disappear (Plate 2d). The stipes of this species are succulent and brittle, hence the name: brittle bladder fern.

Brittle bladder fern *Cystopteris fragilis*

or

Fern with broader, more crowded pinnae (very rare). [2B].

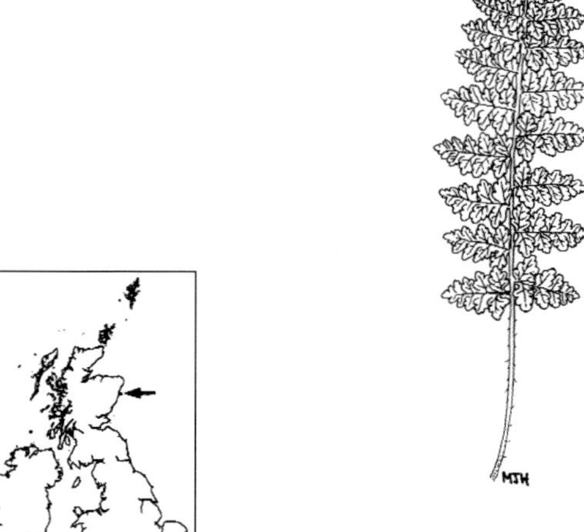

If you have the good fortune to be taken to the little-known sea caves in Kincardine where Dickie's bladder fern is to be found, you will have visited Britain's only known wild site for this fern which resembles the common brittle bladder fern.

Dickie's bladder fern *Cystopteris dickieana*

A fern of rocks, cliffs and shady banks, often near the coast, the frond ovate-lanceolate in outline, narrowing at the base to a pair of inflexed basal pinnae. [2B].

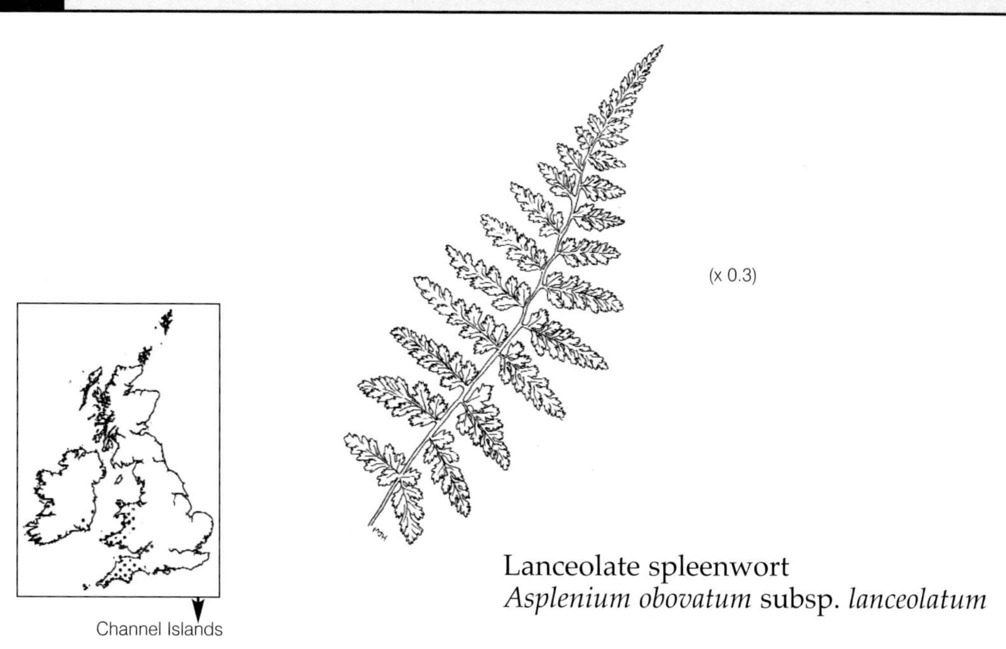

Lanceolate spleenwort
Asplenium obovatum subsp. *lanceolatum*

or

A fern of walls and rocks, inland as well as coastal, the frond triangular in outline, broadest at the base; the stipe is dark brown or black and the basal pinnae are not inflexed. [2/3D].

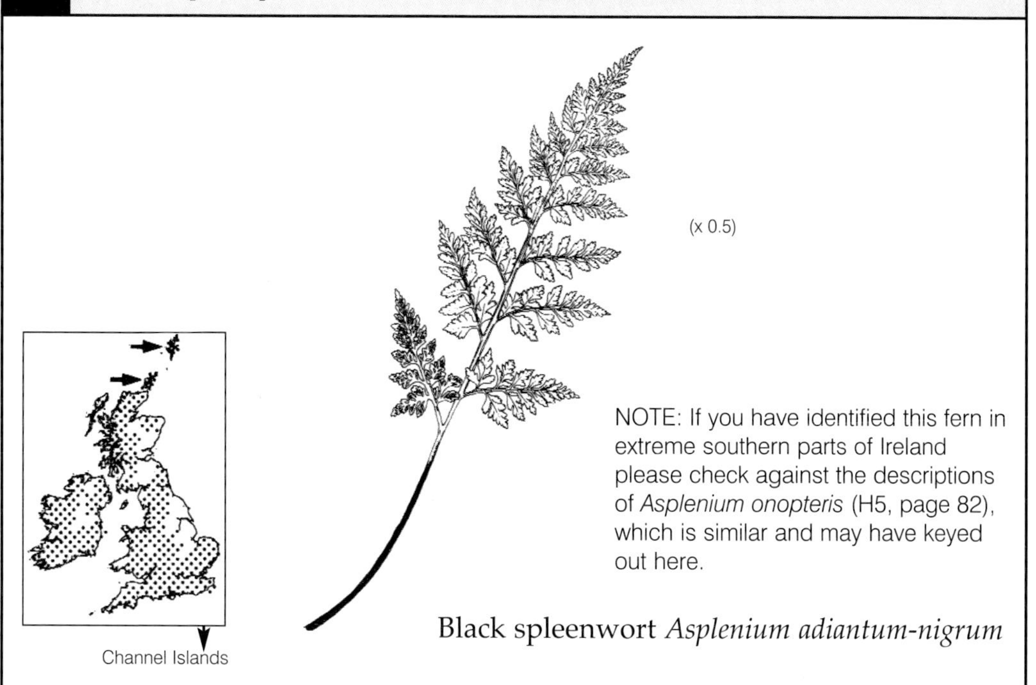

NOTE: If you have identified this fern in extreme southern parts of Ireland please check against the descriptions of *Asplenium onopteris* (H5, page 82), which is similar and may have keyed out here.

Black spleenwort *Asplenium adiantum-nigrum*

G15
↑G8

The pinnules are mitten-shaped in outline, with a prominent 'thumb' lobe at the base, and the pinnule lobes are pointed, many bearing a stiff spike or hair point (2 *Polystichum* species only, opposite).

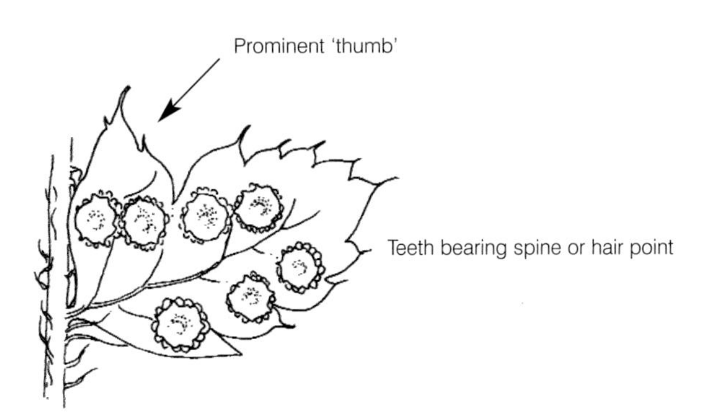

CONFIRMATION: fertile specimens will have sori, the indusia of which will be persistent, circular, centrally attached like minute umbrellas (Plate 3p).

Go to G16, opposite →

or

The pinnules are not distinctly mitten-shaped, and in most (not the male ferns) that prominent 'thumb' is very small or absent. However, the pinnule lobes are no more than serrations, and are never tipped with spines or hairs (13 species in 5 genera).

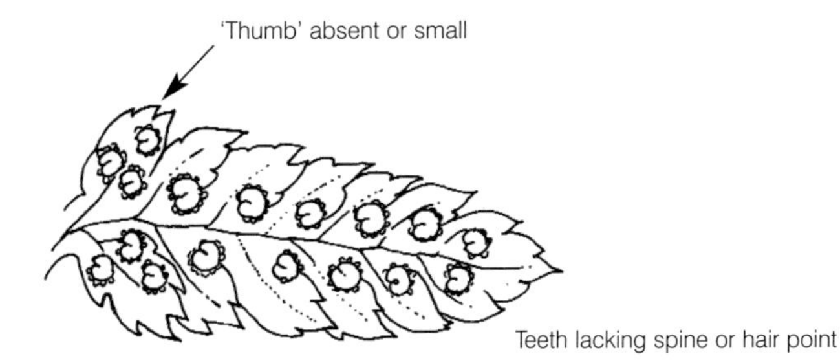

CONFIRMATION: fertile specimens will have sori, the indusia of which will be curved, kidney-shaped or, if circular, are very thin and shrivel early, therefore often apparently absent.

Go to G17, opposite →

G16
↑G15

Refer to Plate 4: larger pinnules have a broad flattened stalk (adnate) whilst smaller ones are unstalked. Pinnule teeth with stiff spines. The pinnule 'thumb' has a ± straight edge and is angled away from the pinna midrib ⓐ. Pinnules become smaller along length of pinna, fusing towards its tip. Angle in the base of many pinnules is acute ⓑ. The frond base is narrower than the mid frond and the stipe less than ⅙ frond length. Grows in the damper parts of woodland on base-rich and calcareous soils and in the grykes of limestone pavement. [2B].

pinnule

NOTE : Young specimens of *Polystichum aculeatum* are frequently mistaken for *P. lonchitis*, the holly fern. However, *P. lonchitis* frequently has sori, even when very small, and the most immature *P. aculeatum* has pinnae which are serrated in such a way as to betray the bipinnateness of future fronds if examined without prejudice of one who desperately wishes to find the rarer species.

(x 0.2)

Hard shield fern
Polystichum aculeatum

or

Refer to Plate 4: most pinnules have a distinct, cylindrical stalk. Pinnule teeth with soft hairs. The pinnule 'thumb' has a rounded edge so that it tends to overlap, or lies more-or-less parallel with the pinna midrib ⓐ. Pinnules become smaller only towards the pinna tip, most of them remaining separate, and many are of equal size. Angle in the base of many pinnules is always obtuse ⓑ. The frond base is approximately as wide as the mid frond and the stipe usually more than ⅙ frond length. Grows in shady hedgerows and the drier parts of woodland on various soils, only rarely in the grykes of limestone pavement. [2B].

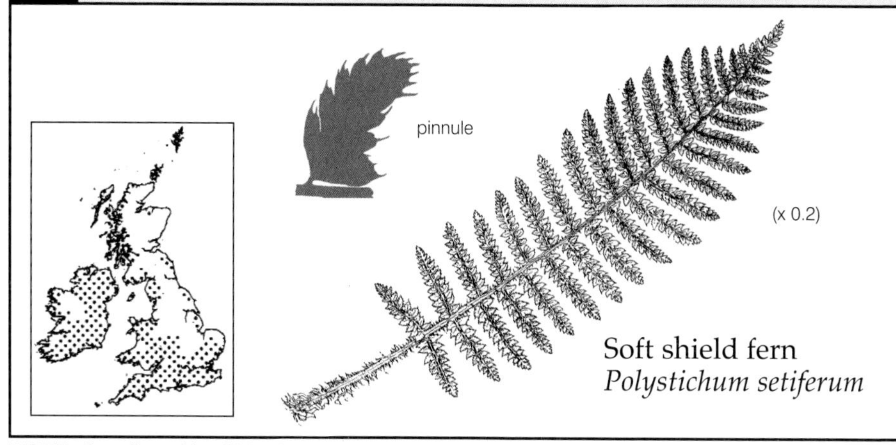

Soft shield fern
Polystichum setiferum

NOTE: 'hard' and 'soft' in the common names of the shield ferns gives an indication of the general texture of the two species. Usually the fronds of *P. aculeatum* are stiff and leathery, indeed quite prickly, whereas those of *P. setiferum* tend to be softer to the touch, the pinnule spines being no more than hairs.

G17
↑G15

The sori are curved (half moon or J-shaped, see Plate 2h, i) the indusium ragged along the free edge. A common delicate woodland, wayside or mountain fern. [2/3B].

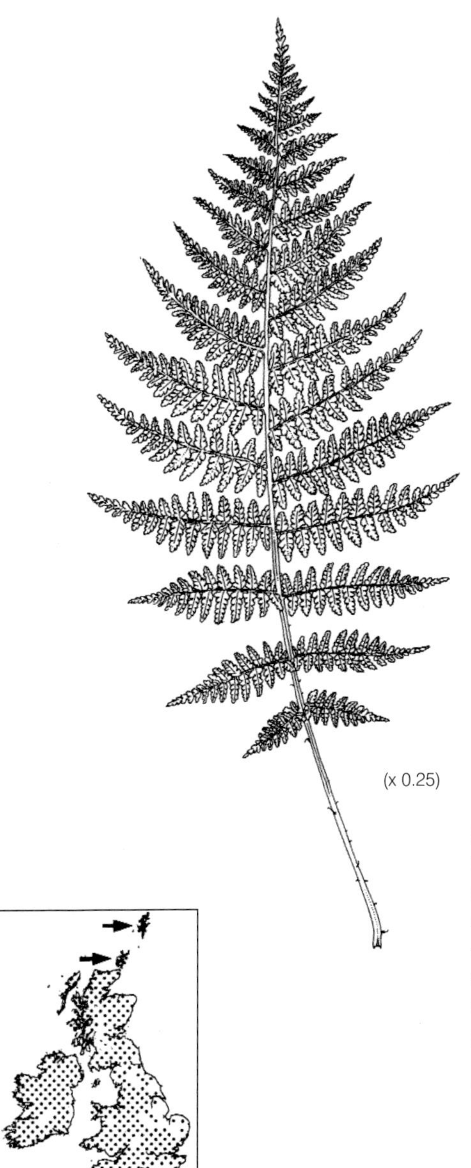

(x 0.25)

Shaded

Open

In shady woodland the fronds of *A. filix-femina* tend to be broad, flat and so delicately dissected as to appear tripinnate. In the open they are coarser and more robust, the pinnules curving so as to have a convex upper surface. The stipe often has a rather succulent appearance and, though usually green, may be wine red in some plants.

NOTE: If you are in high Scottish mountains check *A. distentifolium*, page 72.

Lady fern *Athyrium filix-femina*

Channel Islands

or

The sori are circular or kidney-shaped.

Go to G18, opposite ⟶

G18 **↑G17** The sori are circular or irregular and the indusia ⚲ are either absent or delicate, shrivelling and disappearing early (see Plate 3k).

Go to G19, below

or The sori are kidney-shaped, and although the indusia ⚲ shrivel eventually, many or all remain in place (see Plate 2a).

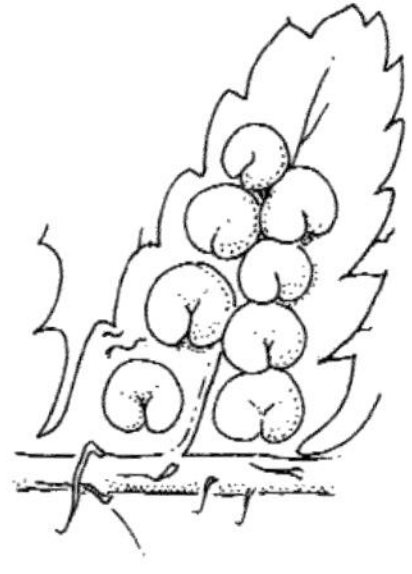

Go to G23, page 73

G19 **↑G18** The fronds grow in lines or apparently at random, actually arising from a creeping rhizome just below or on the soil surface.

Go to G20, overleaf

or The fronds grow clustered around a common point from an upright rhizome.

Go to G21, page 71

G20
↑G19

In woodland or wet rocks and in turf on mountains. Triangular fronds arise from a creeping rhizome. The lowest pair of pinnae are held out and downwards, angled away from the rest. Where the pinnae meet the rachis it is winged in a way not seen in any other British fern. [2C/D].

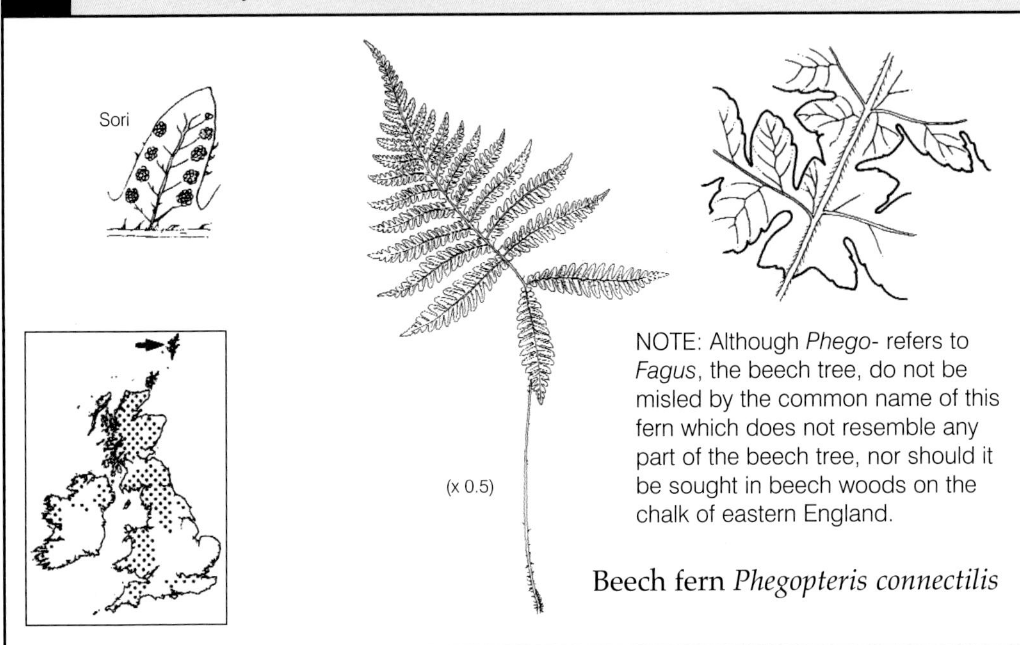

NOTE: Although *Phego*- refers to *Fagus*, the beech tree, do not be misled by the common name of this fern which does not resemble any part of the beech tree, nor should it be sought in beech woods on the chalk of eastern England.

Beech fern *Phegopteris connectilis*

or

In fens. The frond outline is lanceolate to broadly lanceolate, the lower pinnae narrower than those above and not especially angled. [2B].

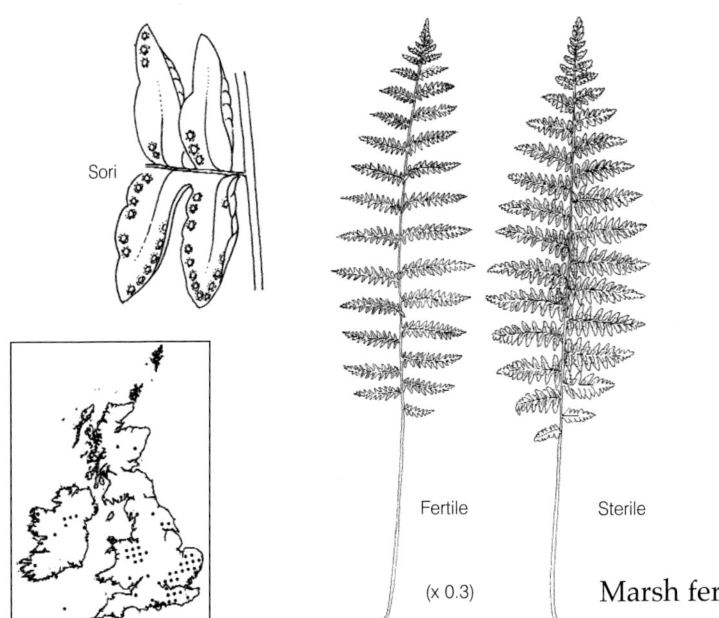

This fern has separate sterile and fertile fronds. The sterile fronds appear in May and are shorter (50-60cm), broader and less upright than the fertile fronds which appear about a month later. These grow up to 80cm tall and the pinna edges tend to roll making them look narrower than those of the sterile fronds.

Marsh fern *Thelypteris palustris*

G21 **↑G19** The pinnule margins are almost entire (unserrated), and lemon-like or citrus scent emanates from crushed young fronds. [2B].

Expanding croziers

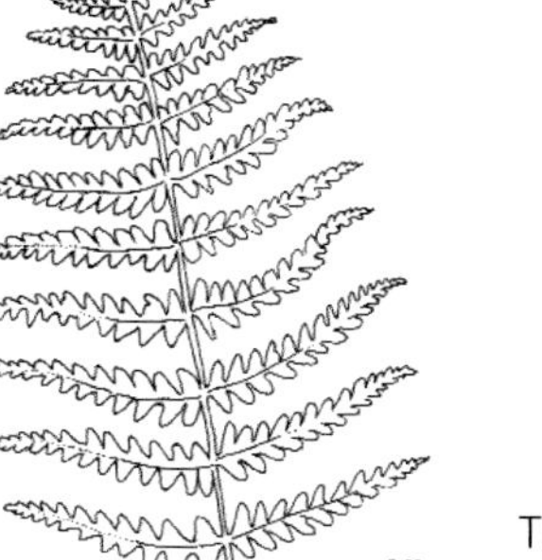

Sori

The sori of *O. limbosperma* are circular and the very thin indusia are visible only early in the season. As the sporangia mature, it shivels and disappears. Sori occupy only the margins of the pinnule undersurface (see Plate 3k). The pinnae decrease in size from mid-frond downward, the lowest being very narrow indeed, a characteristic of no other Britsh fern except *Blechnum*. In a newly expanding frond the young pinnae, which are covered with fine white scales, expand sideways out of the uncurling croziers. Like its common name suggests, it does indeed grow commonly on mountains, but is also an inhabitant of moist, peaty woodland soils in lowland regions.

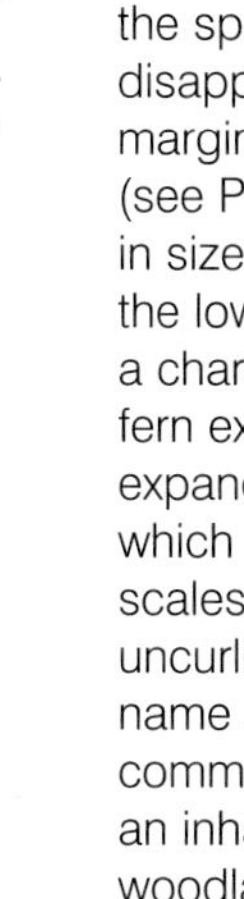

(x 0.3)

Mountain fern (lemon-scented fern) *Oreopteris limbosperma*

or The pinnules are serrated and lack the smell of lemon.

Go to G22, overleaf ------→

G22
↑G21

The fern is found growing on high Scottish mountains; the sori are circular and have no indusium ⚲. [2B].

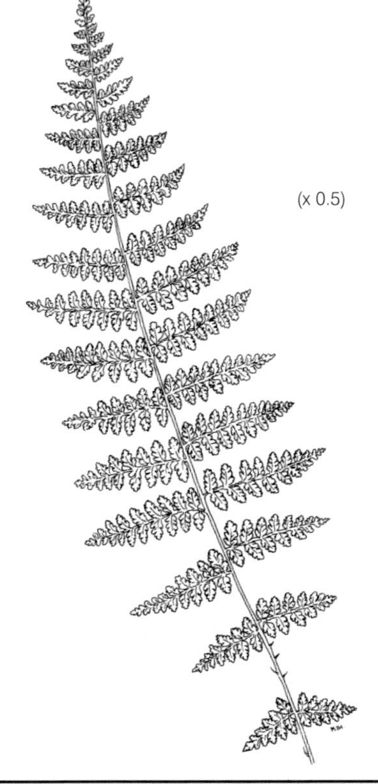

(x 0.5)

The rare alpine lady fern closely resembles the lady fern (G17, page 68). It is very difficult to distinguish high altitude individuals of the lady fern from sterile specimens of the alpine lady fern and sori must be sought for absolute confirmation in the field (the former has J-shaped sori).

Alpine lady fern
Athyrium distentifolium

or

The fern grows as a rather flattened shuttlecock, has a very short stipe and sori are produced only on the lower half of the frond. [2B].

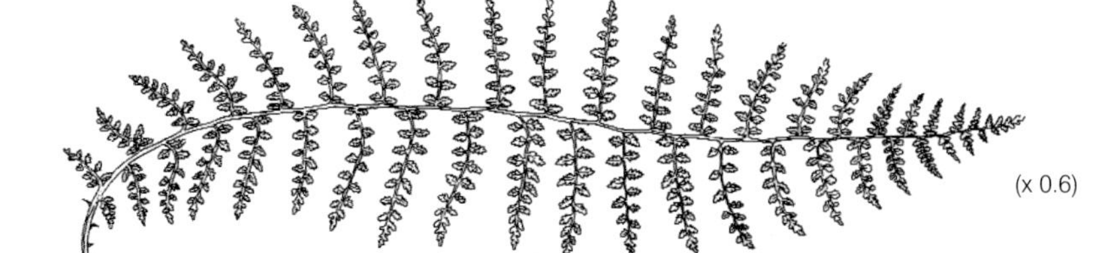

(x 0.6)

This is an unusual fern in that the sori are to be found mainly on the lower pinnae and not in the upper part of the frond. It is a form of the alpine lady fern termed a variety. Varieties of ferns quite frequently occur as isolated individuals (the best are popular with fern-specialist horticulturists) but this one, though rare, occurs relatively frequently and has for many years been considered a distinct species. For these reasons it is usually included in keys when other fern varieties are not.

Flexile lady fern *Athyrium distentifolium* var. *flexile*

G23
↑G18
Grows almost exclusively on the limestone of the Pennines. The fronds are light blue- or grey-green with a mealy surface due to a covering of fine glands 🔍. [2B/C/D].

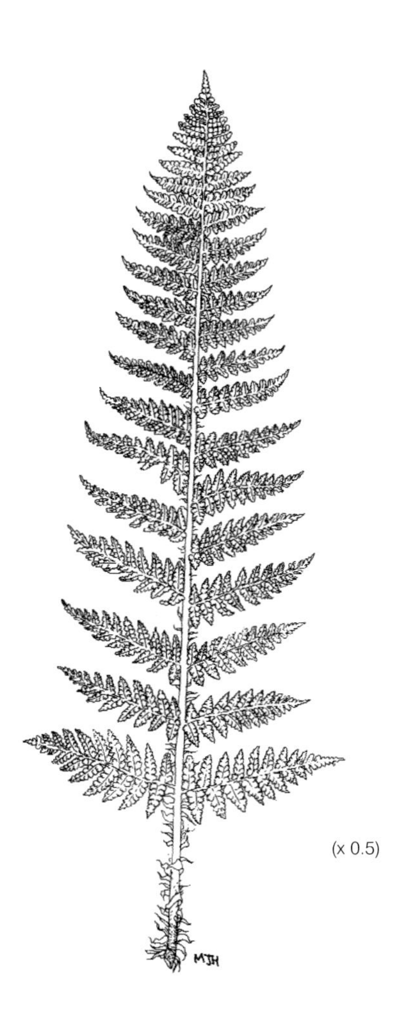

(x 0.5)

Rigid buckler fern *Dryopteris submontana*

or Not on limestone. The fronds are yellow-green to mid green.

Go to G24, overleaf →

G24
↑G23

Grows in East Anglian fens. Very rare. The narrow fronds are light green, the stipe scales never dense or golden and the pinnae are broad and triangular. [2B].

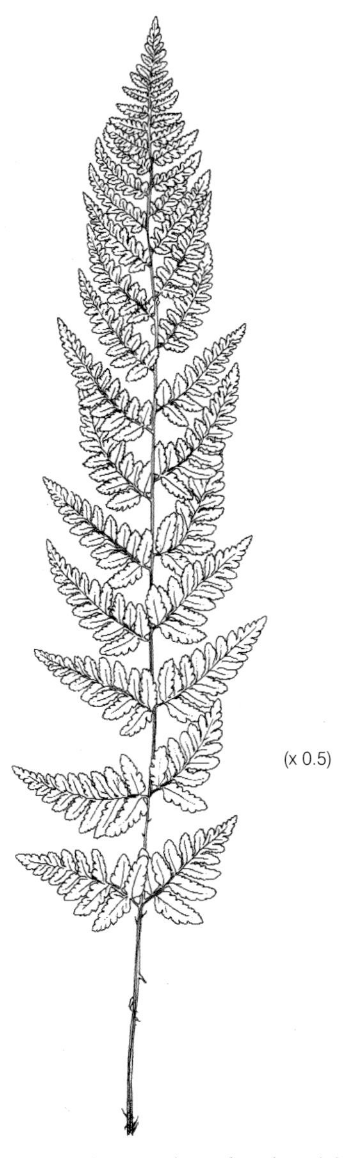

(x 0.5)

Crested or fen buckler fern *Dryopteris cristata*

or

Grows in various habitats (including fens). The fronds are mid-green to golden-green, the stipe relatively densely clothed with scales, and the pinnae lanceolate. One of the five male ferns.

Go to G25, overleaf →

G25-G27 FIVE MALE FERNS

You have reached a stage in fern identification when things start to get a little difficult to say the least. The taxonomy has recently been reviewed and we now have five species. With this key you can stop at 'male fern' or progress further. The degree of your success will be dependent upon the quality of this well-tested key, which certainly has its limitations, and your accumulating experience. Make your choices and take courage; it doesn't get much more difficult than this! See also Plates 6 and 7. The five species are:

Continue overleaf

G25 ↑G24 Brown, black or dark purple at junction of pinna stalk and rachis (often shows at front of frond too). [2B].

Go to G27, opposite

or Green at junction of pinna stalk and rachis (if some darkening here, at back of frond, never visible at front)

Go to G26, below

G26 ↑G25 Pinnules: sides taper towards pointed tip, deeply lobed. Sori: cover more than half of pinnule surface. Indusia: thin, spread loosely at margin and overlap, shrivel completely as spores mature and shed at spore release. [2B].

See Plates 6,7

Common male fern *Dryopteris filix-mas*

or Pinnules: parallel-sided and blunt tipped with inconspicuous blunt teeth. Sori: cover less than half pinnule surface. Indusia: thick, tucked under sporangia at margin, contract as if pulled in by a circumferential drawstring as spores mature and retained after spore release. [2B].

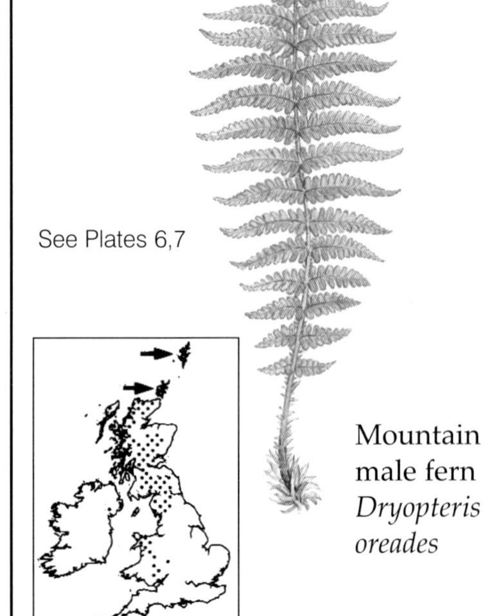

See Plates 6,7

Mountain male fern *Dryopteris oreades*

G27 ↑G25	**or**	**or**
Pinnules: glossy surface, not lobed, parallel-sided with rounded tip bearing inconspicuous, rounded apical teeth. Stipe scales: very dense, rusty to golden. Indusia: thick, tucked under sporangia, split radially as sporangia mature and retained for many years on old fronds. [2B].	Pinnules: dull surface, ± lobed, parallel-sided with square-truncate or round-pointed tip bearing acute apical teeth particularly prominent at the corners. Stipe scales: dense, pale beige. Indusia: thin, tucked under sporangia, roll into a cone as sporangia mature and most are shed at spore release. [2B].	Pinnules: glossy surface, lobed, parallel-sided or tapering to rounded or pointed tip bearing blunt apical 'teeth'. Stipe scales: dense, cinnamon-coloured. Indusia: thick, tucked under sporangia, split or shrivel as sporangia mature and many are retained after spore release. [2B].

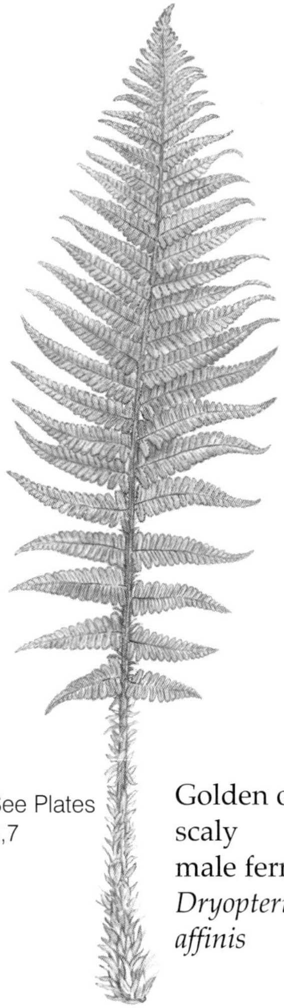

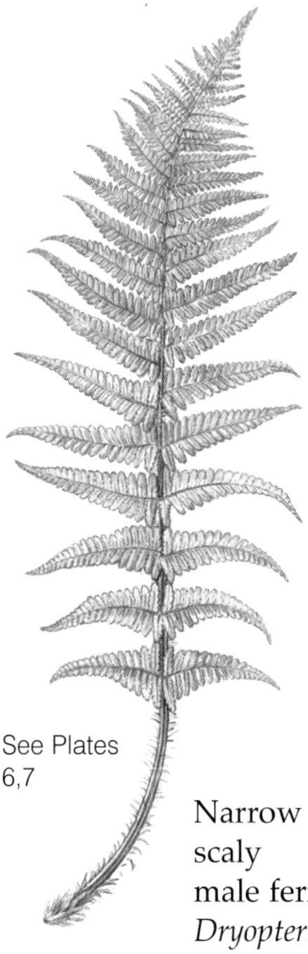

See Plates 6,7

Golden or scaly male fern *Dryopteris affinis*

See Plates 6,7

Borrer's scaly male fern *Dryopteris borreri*

See Plates 6,7

Narrow scaly male fern *Dryopteris cambrensis*

KEY H: FERNS WITH THRICE DIVIDED, TRIPINNATE FRONDS

NOTE: It is possible that finely dissected fronds of the lady fern, *Athyrium filix-femina* (G17), black spleenwort, *Asplenium adiantum-nigrum* (G14), luxuriant examples of the maidenhair fern, *Adiantum capillus-veneris* (G5), Killarney fern, *Trichomanes speciosum* (G2) and large specimens of the brittle bladder fern, *Cystopteris fragilis* (G13) will have been wrongly determined to be tripinnate. They should not resemble the ten ferns shown below. Please back-track.

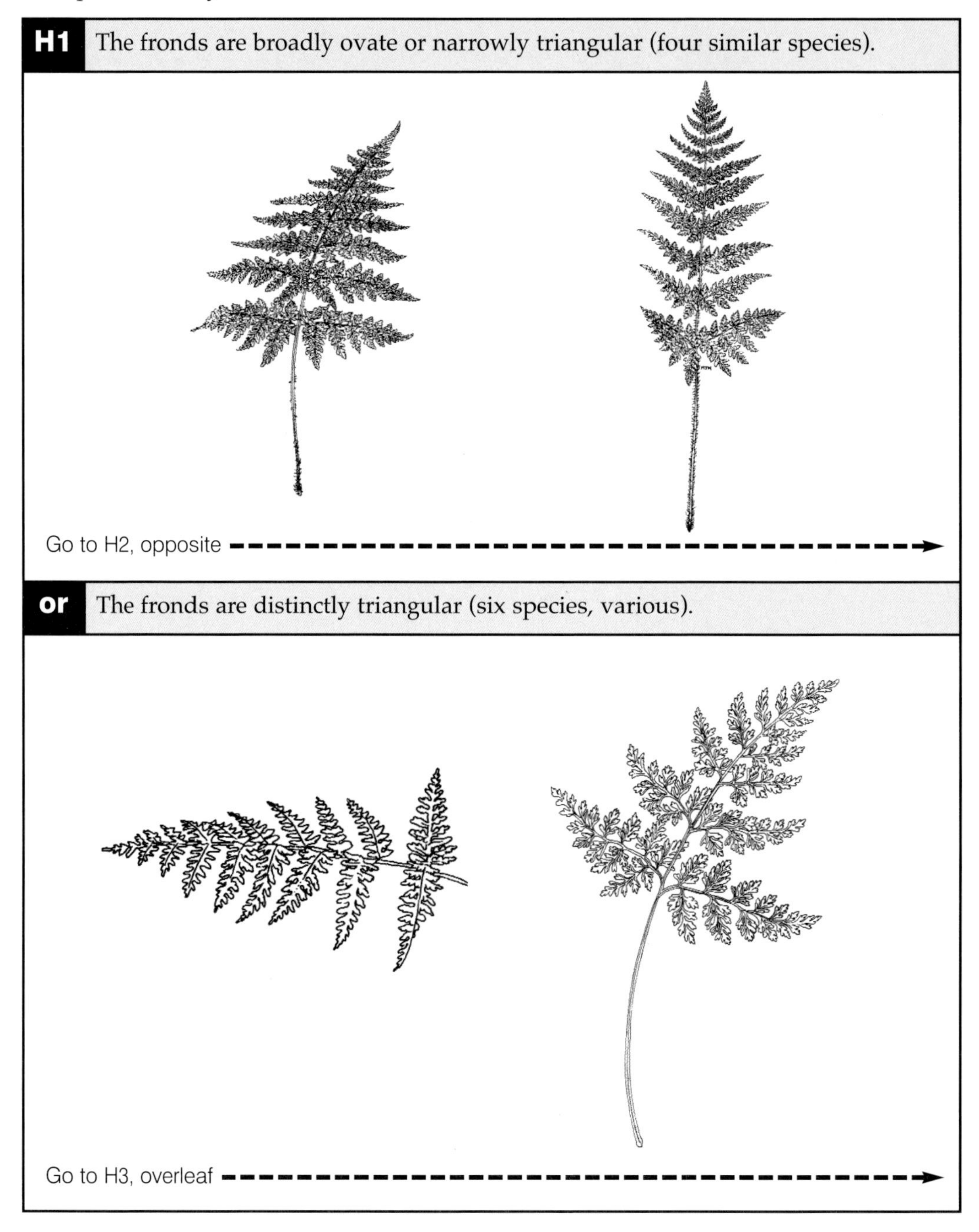

H2
↑H1

Here we encounter an important, but tricky group of ferns in the genus *Dryopteris*. Whereas the male ferns are all bipinnate with lanceolate fronds, these four are tripinnate with almost triangular fronds. A glance at the illustrations will give you an idea of the overall form of the buckler ferns, but attention to detail is the only means of identification. However, as one gets to know these ferns they do become easier to identify at a glance, for habitat, colour, texture and growth form (see below) are all uniquely combined in each of them.

We replace the usual key with a table of characters from which to select the combination to fit the unknown species. Please refer to Plate 5 for illustrations of the details.

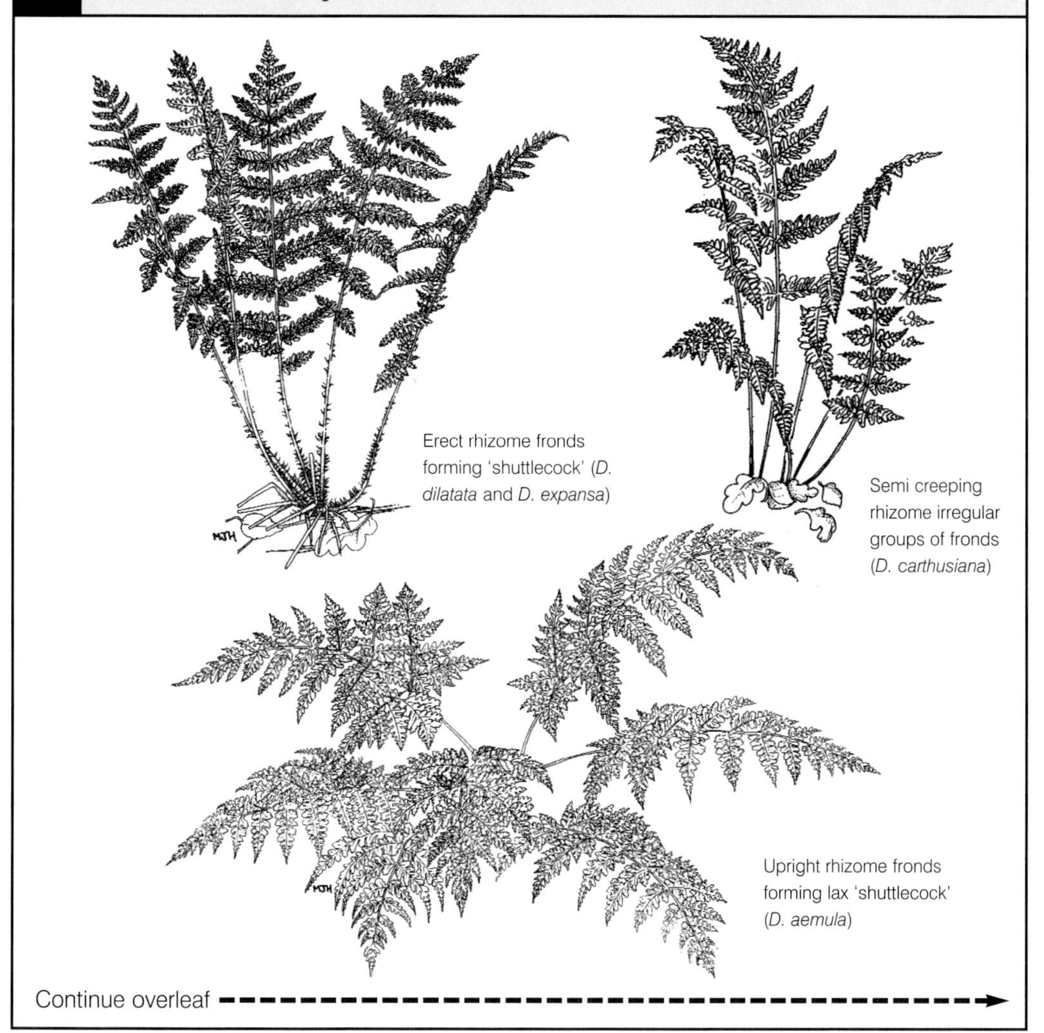

Continue overleaf →

NOTE: *Dryopteris dilatata* and *D. carthusiana* often inhabit adjacent woodland and fenny bog so that their environments grade into one another. Consequently, between the two species, a strip of the hybrid *Dryopteris* x *deweveri* is frequenty discovered. Should you find yourself becoming confused, walk away from your possible hybrid (remembering where you were!) either into dry woodland or towards the wetter land in order to familiarise yourself with reliable features of the parents. When less confused, return to puzzle over the nature of the hybrid zone and its occupants. There are other *Dryopteris* hybrids but they are rarely encountered. Further information may be found in Page (1997).

H2 Continued.

	Broad buckler fern *Dryopteris dilatata*	Narrow buckler fern *Dryopteris carthusiana*	Hay-scented buckler fern *Dryopteris aemula*	Northern buckler fern *Dryopteris expansa*
Growth forms	Upright rhizome. Fronds forming 'shuttlecock'	Semi-creeping rhizome. Fronds in irregular groups	Upright rhizome. Fronds forming lax 'shuttlecock'	Upright rhizome. Fronds forming 'shuttlecock'
Frond attitude	Spreading, facing inwards	Erect, facing randomly	Spreading widely, but facing inwards	Spreading, facing inwards
Frond colour (Guide only)	Dark green	Light green	Light yellow-green	Light green
Scales	Dark stripe down centre	No stripe or patch	Darker concolourous patch at base	No stripe or patch. (Faint stripe in large plants)
Stipe	Dark green with brown-black base	Light green with reddish-brown base	Light green with purplish brown lower third	Light green, brown at very base
Pinnules	Usually curved backwards	Flat (or curved slightly backwards)	Crisped upwards	Flat
Frond type code	3C/D	3C	3C/D	3C/D
Habitat and distribution	Acid woodlands, banks and heaths throughout Britain	Fens and wet woodland throughout Britain	Shady, rocky woodland, western Britain	Sheltered mountain habitats and in woods in mountainous regions, north-west Britain

H3
↑H1

Broadly triangular fronds appear as a single triangle. Three species only, two of which are very rare! (Parsley fern, mountain bladder fern and western black spleenwort).

Go to H4, below

or

Broadly triangular fronds are composed of three, five or more distinct triangles. Three species only (bracken and the two oak ferns).

Go to I1, page 83

H4
↑H3

A small fern with fronds 5-15(-25)cm high, forming tufts or cushions up to 40cm across on non-calcareous mountain screes, crags and walls: the fronds are two distinct types, sterile and fertile. [3D].

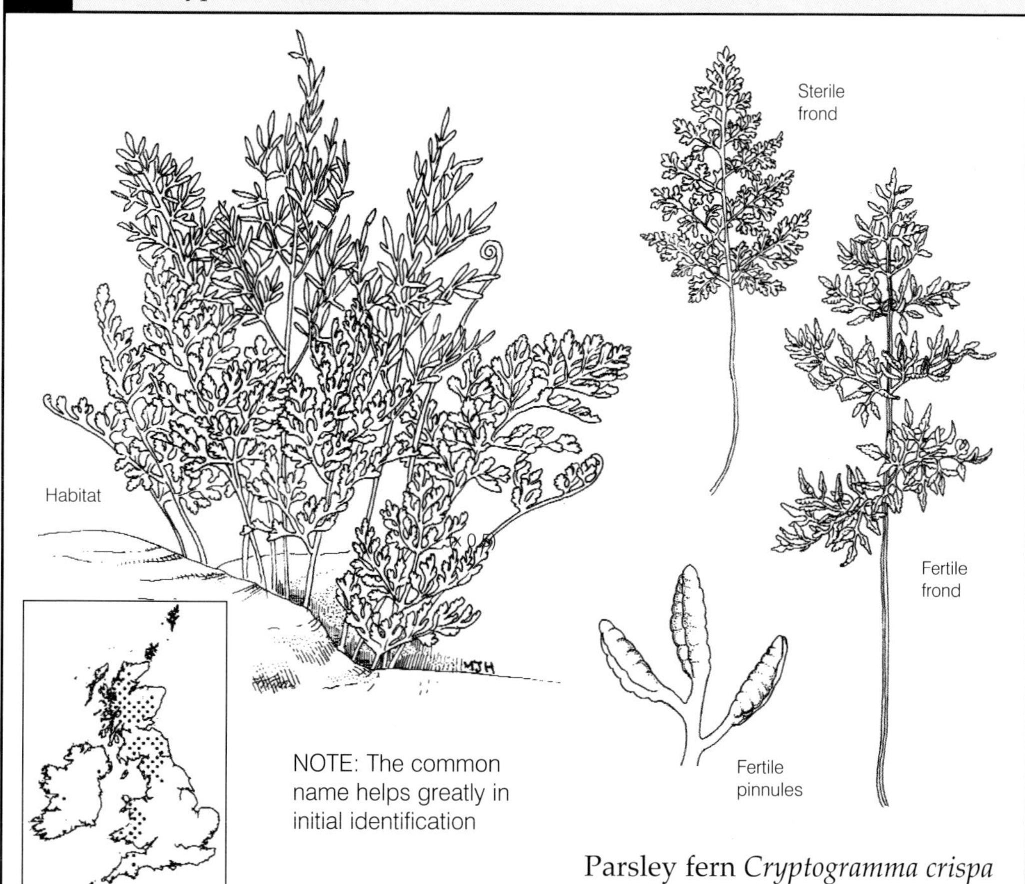

Parsley fern *Cryptogramma crispa*

or

A medium sized fern with fronds exceeding 15cm in height on plants with a creeping or tufted habit.

Go to H5, overleaf

H5
↑H4

If you are looking at the finely-dissected fronds of a fern growing in nutrient rich flushes high on mountains in the central highlands of Scotland (above 750m) you may have the rare mountain bladder fern. Creeping habit. [3D].

or

A rare fern superficially resembling *Asplenium adiantum-nigrum* (page 65) though tripinnate and more finely dissected; grows in the extreme south of Ireland. Tufted habit. [3D].

(x 0.5)

Mountain bladder fern
Cystopteris montana

Asplenium onopteris is a common Mediterranean species of which the Irish population may be a relic from pre-glacial times.

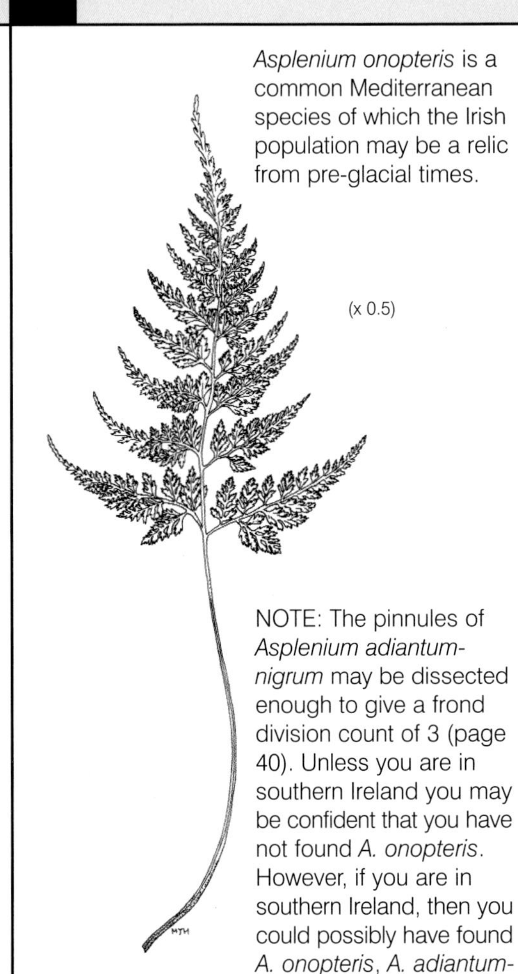

(x 0.5)

NOTE: The pinnules of *Asplenium adiantum-nigrum* may be dissected enough to give a frond division count of 3 (page 40). Unless you are in southern Ireland you may be confident that you have not found *A. onopteris*. However, if you are in southern Ireland, then you could possibly have found *A. onopteris*, *A. adiantum-nigrum* or their hybrid *A.* x *tichense*. Only an experienced eye and laboratory confirmation will tell you exactly what you have found.

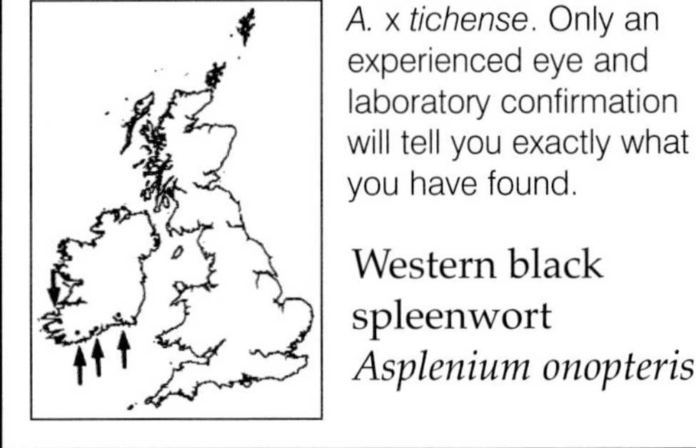

Western black spleenwort
Asplenium onopteris

Key I: British ferns with tripinnate, multipart fronds

I1 A large, robust fern 50-200(-300)cm tall, often spreading over wide areas on mountain or moorland, also an open woodland species. All pinnae except those at frond apex are at least three times divided. [3E].

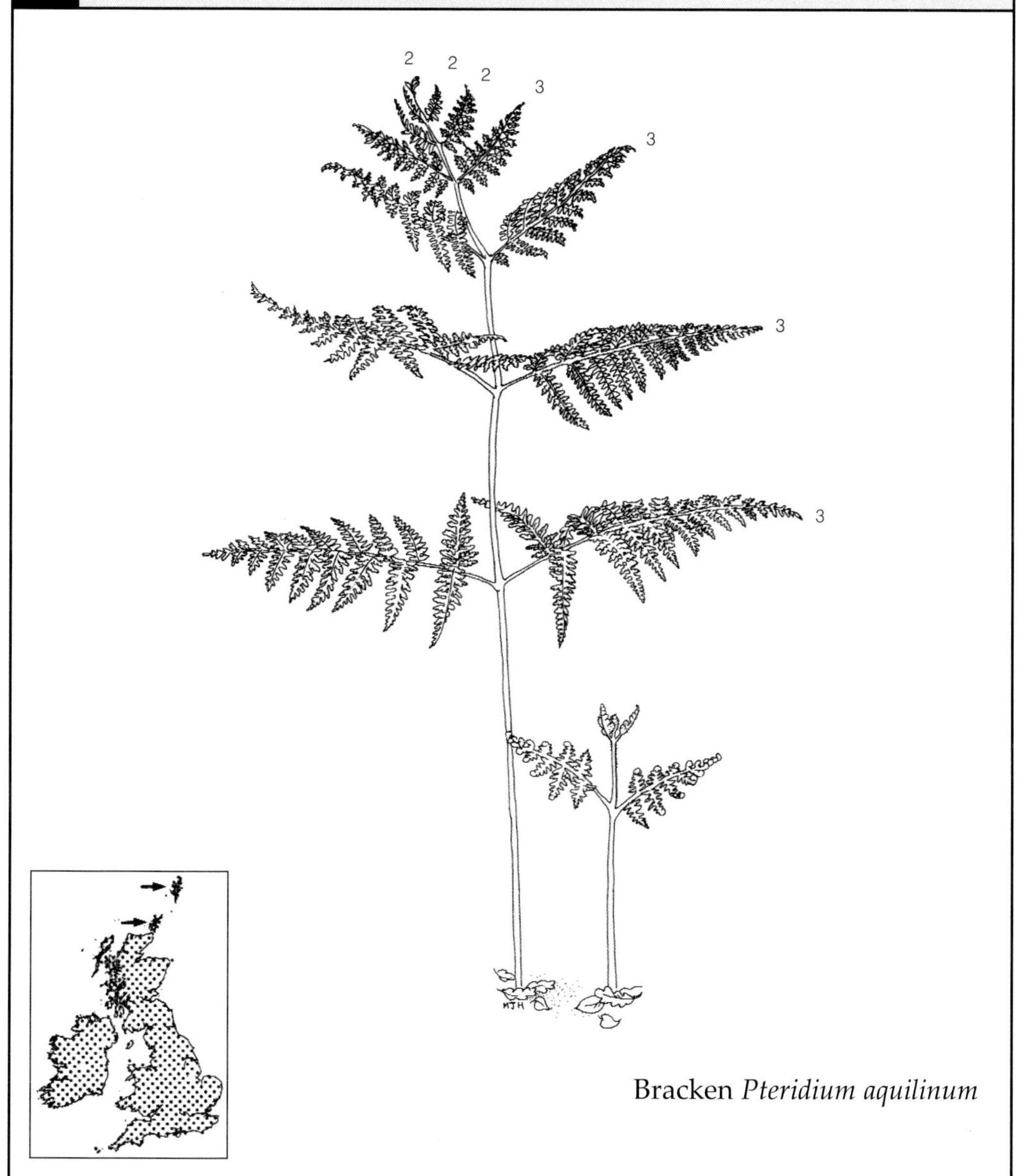

Bracken *Pteridium aquilinum*

or A medium sized fern, 10-40cm tall. Only lowest pair of pinnae are three times divided, the rest twice divided.

Go to I2, overleaf →

I2 **↑I1** A grey-green fern growing in clefts in limestone rocks (occasionally in wall mortar). [3E].

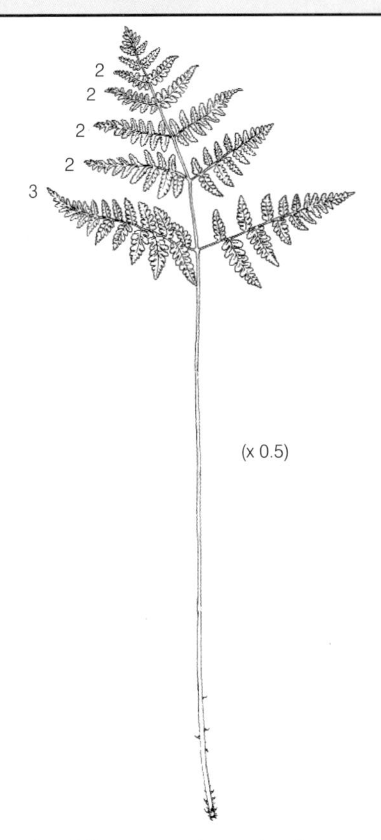

The fronds of *Gymnocarpium robertianum* are covered with minute glands which give it its grey appearance. This is also the case with the rigid buckler fern *Dryopteris submontana* which frequently shares the same habitat. If the fronds of the limestone oak fern are gently brusied a sweet, apple-like scent may be perceived.

Limestone oak fern
Gymnocarpium robertianum

or A light green fern growing in humid rocky woods, on stream banks, on screes but rarely limestone. [3E].

2
2
2
3
(x 0.5)

Gymnocarpium dryopteris differs from its limestone relative, not only in its very different habitat, but also in having no glands on the frond surface (and no apple scent) and the stipe is dramatically bent back to almost 90° at the point of origin of the two lowest (and largest) pinnae.

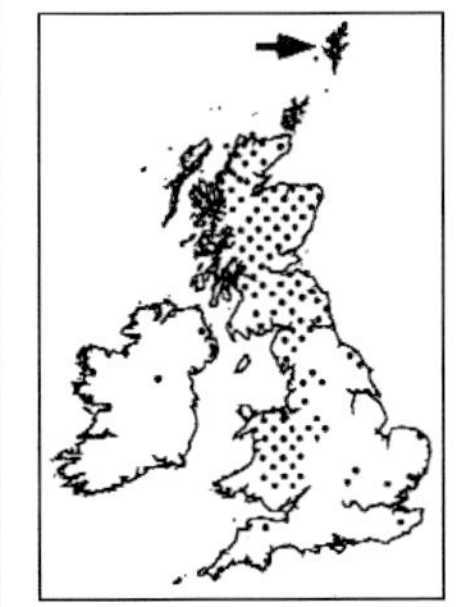

Oak fern
Gymnocarpium dryopteris

NOTE: do not be misled by the common names of the oak ferns which do not resemble any part of the oak tree, but *G. dryopteris* may be found in ravines dominated by oak, especially in the north.

FERNS FOR HOUSE AND GARDEN

The safe future of ferns in the wild is our responsibility, and just going out to dig them up for house and garden will not promote conservation. An acceptable alternative is to propagate them by growing from spores, although it requires a deal of skill and patience, it is by no means impossible. The alternative to growing your own from spore is to purchase ferns ready grown from garden centre or specialist nursery.

Spores may be bought, obtained from the British Pteridological Society's spore exchange or collected in the wild (around mid-summer is the right time for most species – see Plates 2,3 and 7). Put a frond with ripe, but undehisced, sporangia in a labelled envelope and keep it in a dry place until the spores have been released. Many species will keep for years simply left thus until required. However, a few species, especially *Osmunda*, have green spores which will not survive desiccation and must be used at once. While you're waiting for the spores to be released obtain a book about fern culture; those by Jimmy Dyce and Reginald Kaye are excellent (see *Further information*).

When you examine your envelope's contents do not mistake old sporangia for spores. Spores are very, very fine particles. Old sporangia are relatively coarse, granular and roll about. Pour your envelope contents onto a sheet of paper (without the frond) and carefully tilt it so that sporangia roll away leaving the spore dust behind, trapped by the surface fibres of the paper. If it all rolls away you have no spores there – sow empty sporangia and you'll be waiting an eternity for germination!

FURTHER INFORMATION

Camus J., Jermy A.C. & Thomas B.A. (1991). *World of Ferns*. Natural History Museum publications, London.

Clapham A.R., Tutin T.G., [Warburg E.F.] & Moore D.M. *Flora of the British Isles*. (3rd edition). Cambridge University Press, Cambridge.

Dyce J.W. (1988). *Fern Names and their Meanings*. British Pteridological Society, Special Publication No. 2.

Dyce J.W. (1991). *The cultivation and propagation of British ferns*. British Pteridological Society, Special Publication No. 3.

Fitter R. & Fitter A.H. (1984). *The Collins Guide to Grasses, Sedges, Rushes and Ferns of Britain and Northern Europe*. Collins, London.

Hutchinson, G. & Thomas, B.A. (1996). *Welsh Ferns*. National Museum and Galleries of Wales, Cardiff.

Jermy A.C. & Camus J. (1991). *The Illustrated Field Guide to Ferns and Allied Plants of the British Isles*. Natural History Museum publications, London.

Kaye R. (1968). *Hardy Ferns*. Faber and Faber, London.

Merryweather, J.W. (2005). *A Key to Common Ferns*. Field Studies Council, Occasional Publication 94, Shrewsbury.

Merryweather, J.W. (2007). *British Ferns, Clubmosses, Quillworts and Horsetails*. An extensive photographic resource to support identification on DVD. Available from the author (www.merryweather.me.uk).

Page C.N. (1988). *Ferns*. Collins New Naturalist Series, London.

Page C.N. (1997). *The Ferns of Britain and Ireland*. (2nd edition). Cambridge University Press, Cambridge.

Stace C . (1991). *New Flora of the British Isles*. Cambridge University Press, Cambridge.

Wardlaw, A.C. & Leonard, A. eds (2005) *New Atlas of Ferns and Allied Plants of Britain and Ireland*. British Pteridological Society, Special Publication No. 8.

British Pteridological Society. www.ebps.org.uk

Index to species

(a) simple undivided

(b) pinnate once divided

(c) bipinnate twice divided

(d) tripinnate thrice divided

Plate 1. Frond form

(a) *Dryopteris* (see Plate 7)
(b) *Asplenium*
(c) *Asplenium*
(d) *Cystopteris*
(e) *Polypodium* (oval)
(f) *Polypodium* (circular)
(g) *Cryptogramma*
(h) *Athyrium*
(i) *Athyrium*
(j) *Pteridium*

Plate 2. Fern sori

(k) *Oreopteris* (l) *Ophioglossum* (m) *Botrychium* (n) *Hymenophyllum tunbrigense* (o) *Hymenophyllum wilsonii*

(p) *Polystichum* (q) *Blechnum* (r) *Gymnocarpium* (s) *Osmunda*

Plate 3. Fern sori (continued)

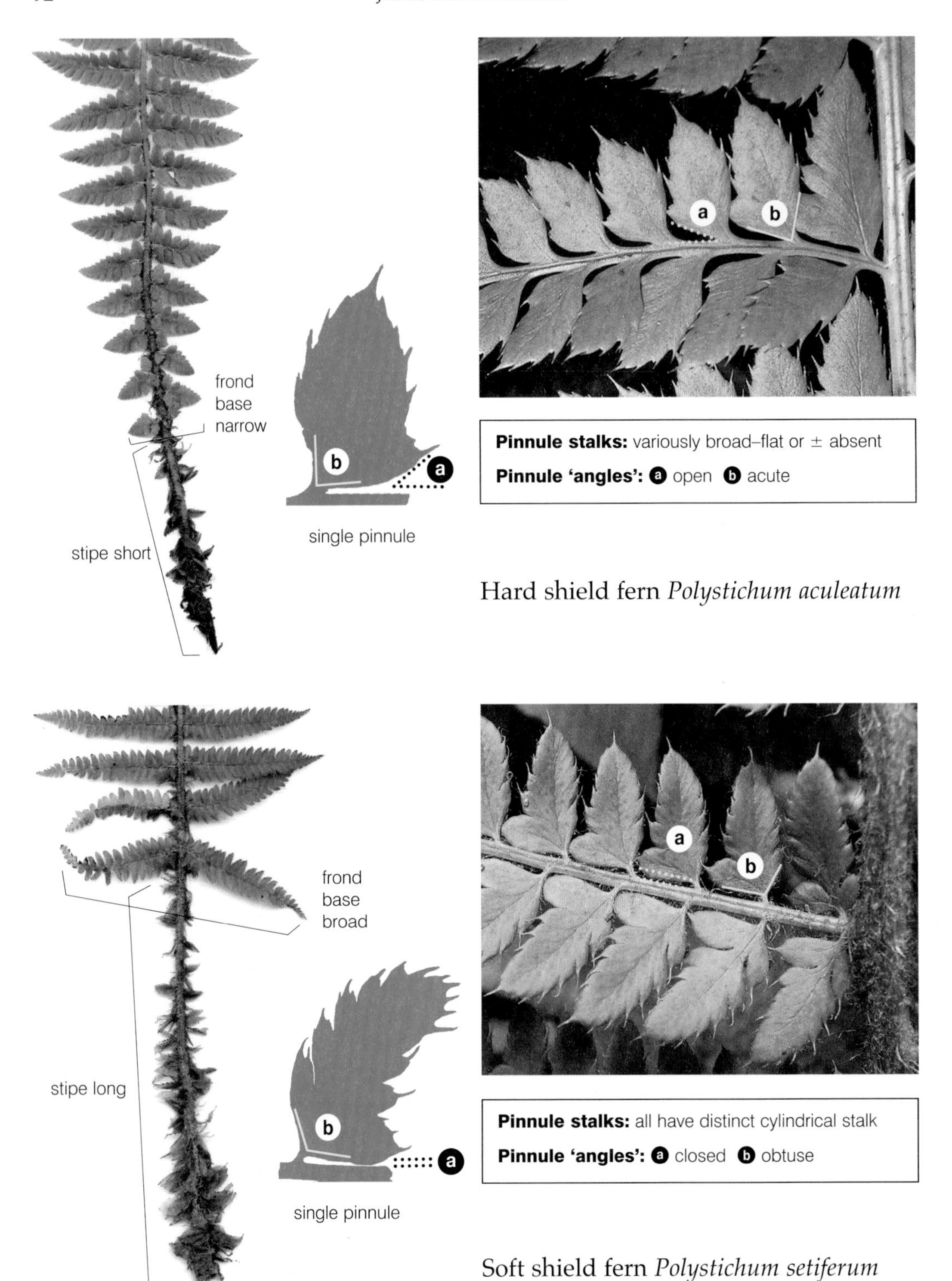

Plate 4. Two shield ferns, *Polystichum* spp.

Plate 5. Four buckler ferns, showing fronds, pinnules and stipe scales.

Plate 6. Five male ferns, showing frond and pinna.

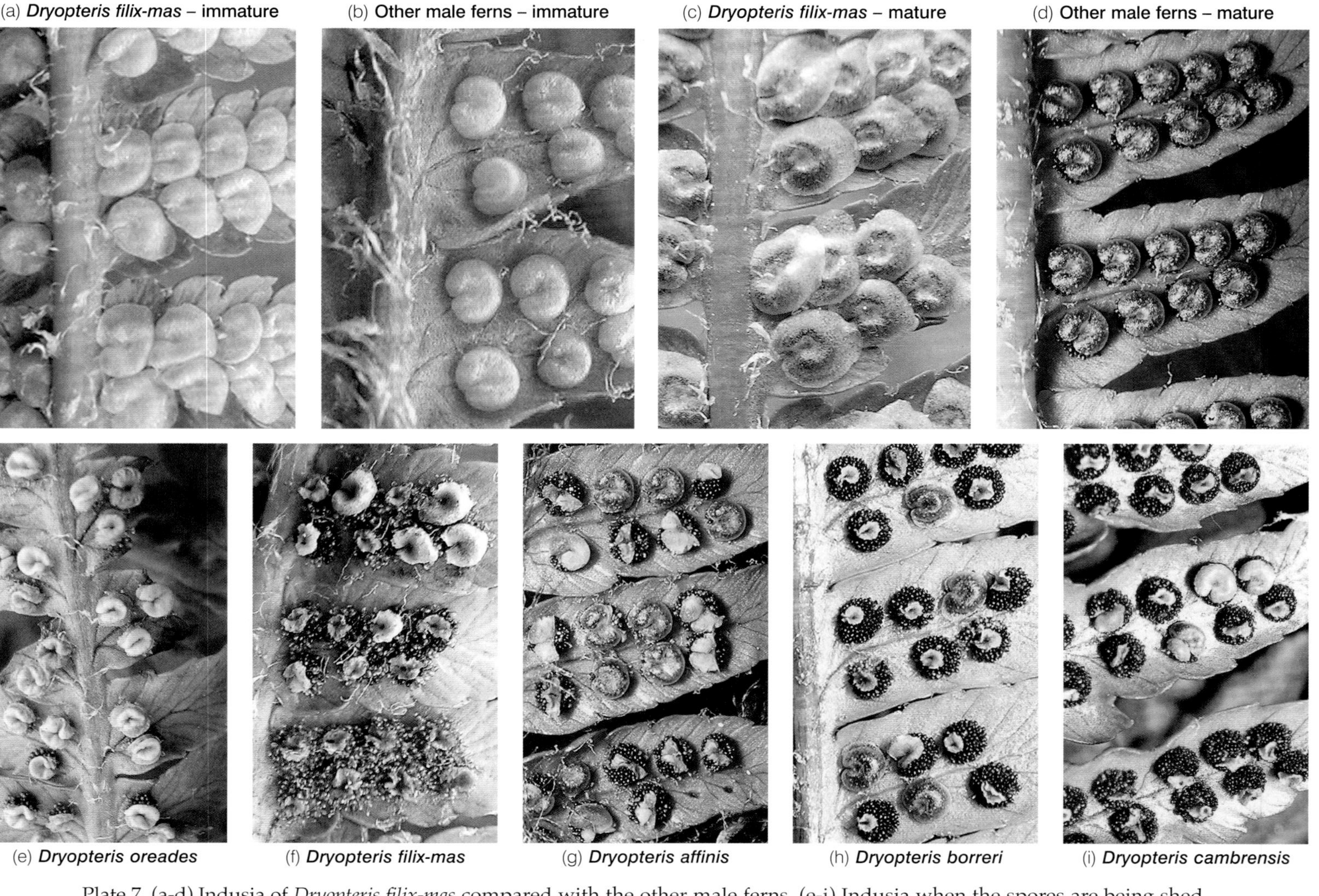

Plate 7. (a-d) Indusia of *Dryopteris filix-mas* compared with the other male ferns. (e-i) Indusia when the spores are being shed.

Plate 8. Two filmy ferns (*Hymenophyllum* spp.)